JEALOUS OF THE DEAD

Secrets of an Immigrant Survivor

ALDIANA PEHLIVANOVIĆ DEUMIĆ

Published by Aldiana Pehlivanović Deumić Morton Grove, Illinois

This memoir reflects the author's personal recollections and experiences, viewed through the lens of a child. The events and reflections are the author's subjective interpretations and are not intended to represent the perspective or experience of others. To protect the privacy and anonymity of individuals, names and identifying details have been changed. Any resemblance to actual persons, living or dead, is coincidental and not intended to cause harm.

First Print Edition in the United States of America by Aldiana Pehlivanović Deumić, 2025

Library of Congress Control Number: 2025916900

ISBN E-Book: 979-8-9997531-1-3

ISBN Paperback: 979-8-9997531-0-6

ISBN Hardback: 979-8-9997531-2-0

Graphic Design and Editing: Jessica D. Ashdown of Jessica Diane Consulting

Book Cover Co-Designer: Selma Muminović

Formatting: Alina Rubin of Hearts and Sails Author Services

Contents

I *am tired of living, though I've barely lived. Tired of hoping, though I've hardly hoped. Tired of speaking, though I've spoken little. Tired of remembering, though I've forgotten much. Tired of everything, except sleep.*

— Meša Selimović, The Dervish and Death

ACKNOWLEDGEMENT

To my husband Amir and my daughters Almedina and Aminela, thank you for your patience, support, and unconditional love. Your endless listening, honest feedback, and encouragement carried me through the hardest parts of this journey.

To my parents, sister, aunts, uncles, cousins, and lifelong friends, thank you for giving me strength and roots, and for patiently listening to this story over the years—even when it was hard to share.

To my editor and publishing consultant, Jessica D. Ashdown of Jessica Diane Consulting and author of *God Is With You When*, thank you for your invaluable support and guidance. Your mentorship brought this story to life and reminded me that hope endures even in moments of doubt.

To Alina Rubin, author, speaker and entrepreneur of *Hearts and Sails Series*, thank you for being my book formatter and sharing your expertise.

This book carries the weight of many lives. I am proud to share their stories.

DEDICATION

To the victims, the survivors, the children of Bosnia and Herzegovina, and the generations who carry the memory forward — may your pain be remembered, your courage respected, and your stories never forgotten.

To the children of Gaza.

To refugee and immigrant children.

To those with invisible wounds — depression, anxiety, PTSD, and neurodivergent conditions.

To everyone who has envied the dead at least once in their life but kept on breathing. Who survived, even when they weren't sure they wanted to. Who, despite everything, found a reason to stay.

Your pain is not invisible.

Your story is important.

You are the light that survives the darkness.

PROLOGUE

I was nine years old when the war came for my family in Žepče, Bosnia. I didn't know then how far the war's shadow would stretch—across continents, years, and generations.

In 1993, we were forced into camps—detention sites that included the Nova Trgovina Camp, hangars, where women, children, elderly, the sick, my mother, sister, grandparents, aunts, and my handicapped uncle were imprisoned. The so-called "silos," the Rade Kondić school, which was my elementary school where I completed first grade before the war began, and the primary school in Perković Han were also places of captivity. These were not formal institutions, but brutal, makeshift facilities controlled by combat forces. We lost neighbors, family, and the fragile innocence of childhood.

Today, in 2025, thirty-two years later, in my hometown of Žepče, there are still no clear or officially recognized markers indicating the locations of those former detention centers and concentration camps. What is even more heartbreaking is that many Muslim Bosnians—or Bosniaks as we were called—who survived the war in Žepče and were imprisoned in these sites remain uncertain about the legally recognized names used in official United Nations and International Criminal Tribunal records. It is painfully clear that some would prefer us to forget what happened and erase the memory of a cruel past.

This story is not just about war. It is not just about Bosnians, Serbians, and Croatians. It is about what comes after war: silence, survival, split self.

By the time we made it to the United States, we were no longer just Bosnians—we were refugees, immigrants, outsiders.

In America, I quickly learned that survival required shapeshifting. My name was too long, too foreign. Kids turned it into a punchline—Aladdin, Aldi-market, terrorist. My accent betrayed me before I even opened my mouth. I did not understand why I was so different, only that I was. Being different meant being wrong, being mocked, being erased. So, I hid the shame of being "other" behind perfect grades and practiced smiles.

As a teenager, I was always strong, always capable. I smiled. I got straight A's. I translated bank statements and court letters. I filled out school forms and job applications for my parents. I raised my younger sister when my mother could not. I was the parent of the parents. I held everyone together like glue.

But behind my smile lay generations of history, exile, fear, pain, and illness—silent and festering. I carried secrets, some inherited, some born from survival, some self-inflicted. I never asked for help. I never learned to say no. I never learned to set boundaries or to prioritize my own needs because being the "good Bosnian girl" was what people needed from me.

What no one saw were the scars I carried—genetic, generational, and situational. PTSD, depression, anxiety, and a nervous system always on high alert.

Sometimes, I wished I could disappear. I thought about ending my life more than once. But I didn't. I kept smiling. Kept performing strength.

Kept pretending I knew how to pray when I didn't—because nobody taught me how. I didn't know who I was allowed to become, only who I was expected to be.

I began writing this story thirty years ago in the form of a journal. Back then, the words were only for me—a way to survive, to make sense of a world that had torn itself apart.

This memoir—*Jealous of the Dead: Secrets of an Immigrant Survivor*—is a more raw, more complete version of the book I first wrote under the title *Through Darkness: A Story of the Bosnian Diaspora*, which was endorsed by the Illinois Holocaust Museum.

Some names in this book are real, while others have been fictionalized or changed to protect the privacy, safety, and legality of the people in these pages. Some characters are described without names for the sake of clarity and simplicity—not because they are unimportant. I honor and thank every person described here. I am deeply grateful to all of them and approach their stories with the utmost respect.

It has taken me years to feel ready to share the full story. Healing is not linear. It is slow, uneven, and sometimes nearly unbearable.

I am no longer writing from the numbness of survival but from the clarity that comes with pain acknowledged.

I wrote this not just for myself but for every refugee teenager who could not explain why they were so angry, so sad, so quiet, or so loud. For the immigrant girls who feel too much and belong nowhere. For the children of war who survived—but carry the war inside them still.

I wrote this not to reopen wounds but to remind us that scars mean we survived—and surviving means we still have the power to speak, to heal, and to remember.

PART ONE: I Am From Bosnia

1

Even Bosnian Girls Have Secrets

Žepče, Bosnia and Herzegovina – June 1993

Sometimes I wish I were a ghost. Not dead—just invisible. Like mist that slips through cracks and doesn't have to hear bombs, shouting, or the secrets people stuff in their pockets.

I'm nine years old. We're packed like sardines in the basement of our house—about fifty people crammed into this tiny space for almost a week. Family, relatives, neighbors, other refugees. The air is thick and heavy with dust, sweat, and fear. The smell of old bread mixes with the cold damp moisture that seeps through the cracked concrete walls. There's no electricity, no running water, no shower—only one toilet down the hall. We sleep on cardboard boxes and thin, worn blankets spread over the cold floor. The walls creak like they might cave in any second.

I share this dark, hollow space with my sister Arijana, Mama, aunts, cousins, neighbors and refugees from surrounding cities and villages. Outside, the war echoes above our heads—distant gunfire, planes roaring, neighbors whispering secrets that curl around the shadows.

I don't pray. Not because I don't want to. But because I don't know how. My two grandmas, Nana Điha and Majka Zulka, pray quietly. I watch Nana and Majka when they think no one's looking—their lips moving fast, their hands rising, their whole bodies softening like they're talking to someone kind. Someone who listens. I try to copy them sometimes, mouthing the syllables, bowing my head like I've seen them do. But the words don't feel right in my mouth. My tongue trips, and I feel fake. Like even God would see through me and say, *Oh come on, Aldijana, stop pretending. You don't even know how to pray. You act like you've memorized surahs in front of Muslims and then tell Croats and Serbs your dad is a communist.*

Mama says we're Muslims. Tata, my dad, says, "She can speak for herself." He's an atheist. A communist. He rolls his eyes when Mama talks about God. "If God existed, we wouldn't be hiding in a damn basement," he mutters, like it's a punchline—but nobody laughs.

Even before the war, their fights would start quietly. A sigh. A mutter. Then boom—just like the war above us:

"You're just like your mother, you never shut up," Tata growled.

"And you! You're just like your father. Hardheaded, big ego. Always trying to control everything and everyone. Always wanting the last word. You make everyone fear you somehow," Tata snorted. He would slam the door open so hard the walls shake. I would jump a little and hold my breath, afraid to move. I would shut my eyes and make up fairy tales in my head about princesses, pretending I'm somewhere else.

My grandfather, Dido Avdo, Tata's father, died of throat cancer from smoking and drinking too much. I never met him. Nana says he once brought home another woman he never married. Thankfully, she didn't stay.

If you ask me, no one's an angel. Mama and tetka— my aunt—used to whisper about their dad, Dido Hašim, and his "bastard child." I didn't

9

really know what that meant, but it sounded bad—like something you definitely don't want to be. They said it happened before he got married to Majka, maybe while he was watching cows or goats or something. They never said that stuff at dinner, but I heard it anyway.

Because my secret is this: I listen. I observe. I see. I hear. I spy. I act innocent. And I learn. I learn there are no angels, only secrets.

I stay up to hear them fight. I keep still when they talk about forbidden things. I press my body into the walls and let their anger fill the space between my ribs. I know things kids aren't supposed to know. And honestly? That makes my boring life feel a little less boring.

But some things—names, stories—are too dangerous to ask about. So, I listen. And try not to exist too loudly.

When it gets too much—the yelling, the waiting, the war—I hurt myself.

Not in big ways. In small, quiet ones. I chew the inside of my cheeks until they taste like rust. I peel the skin around my fingernail until it bleeds. I walk into door frames on purpose, letting my shoulder slam into a corner. I bruise easily, and I press down on those bruises just to feel something I can control.

I rock back and forth. Again and again. Until the people and furniture in the room sway with me. My head grows heavy. The floor is cold, but I don't feel it anymore.

When I'm not hurting myself, I hold Teddy. I press his fuzzy body against my ear. I whisper, "I'm scared." He doesn't answer. But he never leaves.

Now we're all holding our breath, afraid to move, and longing for the weeks before when we could express ourselves.

The basement walls creak. The air is thick with sweat, fear, and old bread. Fifty of us are crammed in here. We haven't showered in weeks. Can't go upstairs. Can't make noise.

We're hiding from the Croats now.

Before the bombs started falling, everyone said this war wasn't real. That Croats were different. Better. Not like the Serbs. The Serbs were already scary. People whispered about them burning towns, taking dads away.

But Croats? They were our neighbors. Classmates. Friends. They came over for coffee. Brought cake. Shared snacks at school.

That's what makes it worse.

This doesn't feel like war. It feels like betrayal. Like someone handing you a slice of bread with one hand, then stabbing you with the other.

We huddle under blankets. Recite Quran verses. Pretend not to hear the screams above us. Dust falls from the ceiling with every explosion. It rains indoors.

Sometimes I pee myself in my sleep. I don't care. Mama doesn't yell. She hands me fresh clothes and keeps my secrets. I wrap myself in my red flower blanket and curl up on the cold cement floor.

If Teddy was real, he'd rage at the ceiling. Demand answers from God. Scream back at the guns. But he's not. So, I scream silently. All I want is quiet. To not shake. To not smell gunpowder and pee and shame. To see sunlight. To feel clean.

To believe Tata will avenge us like Bruce Willis in one of those loud American movies, covered in sweat and glory, saving everyone just in time.

But the bombs keep falling. The basement keeps filling. And sometimes—when it's all too dark, too loud, too heavy to carry—I secretly hurt myself.

Not because I want to die. But because then I don't want to be afraid anymore. I want to feel in charge.

2

Hide and Seek

Žepče, Bosnia and Herzegovina – June 30, 1993

"Please don't do it!" mother's voice cracks, her hands trembling, as she takes the matches from my father's cracked dry hands.

"What's happening?" My sister and I ask, both of us lost and scared.

My curls are wet, my chest feels tight, like there's weight pressing down.

To my right, I see my mother and my father's mother, Nana Điha, both on their knees crying hard, gasping for air between sobs. My mother hugs my father like this will be the last time she can. My Nana, her tiny hands worn thin from years of grief, clings to his hand, refusing to let go.

Arijana's small body shakes next to me, her baby teeth clenched tight, as if she's trying to hold back fear.

"Dad, please stop! You are scaring us." My sister and I beg, tears pouring down our faces.

I have seen my father angry before, but this isn't him.

"Senada, please talk to him. Don't let him burn down our home," my Nana cries out, her voice broken.

I lean close to Arijana and I whisper in her ear, "Ari, let's play hide-and-seek underneath my blanket. It'll be okay."

"Aldi, is Dad really going to burn down our house? Where will we hide? Where will we live?" Ari looks at me with her puppy face and pale skin, like she's seen a ghost.

"Of course he's not. He's not a bad guy. Only bad guys do such things. Let's go play now," I say, trying to sound convincing, even though I'm not sure I believe myself.

"I DON'T WANT TO!" she yells, stomping her foot hard against the floor. "You're not the boss of me!" she snaps, pushing me with her thin arms. This isn't the first time she's done this.

I want to shove her back, but I stop myself. There's enough fighting around me already. Besides, I'm older, taller—I could push her down, but it wouldn't make anything better.

I glance around the room and see my mom holding Tata's feet, begging him to calm down.

"Let me go. Pustite me!" Father demands to be let go, his voice shaking with rage and his hands pushing my Mama's away as if she's trying to hurt him.

"Nemoj molim te. Smiri se. Misli na djecu," mother tries to reason with him to calm down and to think of us, his children.

"If anyone is gonna burn down our home, that will be me. My sweat! My money! My house! My rules!" Father continues.

"Sine moj, nemoj molim te," my old Nana Điha asks Tata the exact thing Mama just did. No luck. His mind seems to be made up. I'm not surprised. He's the boss of our house. Mama says Tata is a proud man. Hardheaded, with a big ego who doesn't like to lose. I understand the meaning of the word proud, and not liking to lose, but what on earth is ego?

I take several deep breaths, the kind we learned at school to help when we're upset. I breathe in through my nose, hold it, and then exhale through my mouth, trying to calm the tight knot in my chest. This relaxes my nerves a little and prevents me from starting another war.

Hide-and-seek has always been our favorite game especially when Mama runs after us to teach us a lesson. This is the first time Ari said no when I asked her to play. Because she can be so annoying, I avoid playing with her. Anytime we play, one of us ends up crying, and then we both get in trouble with Mama or Tata. Sometimes, Mother sends us outside to pick a motka—a wooden stick—to teach us a lesson. If she's really angry, or if she's in a rush, her hand does the job. It can leave red marks on our cheeks or butt. Father's way of discipline is more military style. Stand still. Listen to his long lectures. Accept the consequences. Serve your time. But on the worst days, when Mama and Tata are both angry—Father uses the belt. Not often. Just enough to make us remember.

"Leave me alone! I want my Mama," Arijana continues to scream at me. I swear to God, this girl gets on my nerves so much. Oftentimes, I have to walk away to cool down or else I'll punch her in her face. *How can she be so selfish? It's my Mama, too!*

At this point, I don't care. I'm not her mother and I shouldn't be the adult here. My hands keep squeezing into fists like they have their own anger. I get up and walk away. Anger boils inside me, waiting to strike something that won't cry back. I take my pink teddy bear and I shove my face into him. I scream as loud as I can, hoping no one will hear me in the madness of this place.

Suddenly, there's silence. Everyone is staring at me now. Mama is rubbing Arijana's back and she has her on her lap. Ari is such a baby. And a mama's girl. I want Mama to rub my back and put me on her lap. I need comfort too.

Without thinking, my Speedy Gonzalez feet run to Tata. I hug him with all my strength as if this is the last time I'll ever see him. His heart is pounding against mine, and mine is beating just as fast. I pull down my hoody and I wipe his forehead with it, my hands shaking. Neither one of us speaks. He runs his right hand through my curls, slow and gentle, like he's trying to calm me. I wish we could stay like this forever. Even if he's sweaty.

Even if it means another lecture, motka, a hand, or a belt—I'd still rather be with Mama and Tata than go to a concentration camp. At least the beatings come with a roof, warm food, and someone yelling that they love you. We're hiding now. But what happens when they find us?

3

Monsters and Momsters

Žepče, Bosnia and Herzegovina – June 30, 1993

Now that we're about to be locked behind barbed wire, everything starts to make sense. In April 1993, news came, then silence. At the end of first grade, our Serbian teacher left—with no goodbye, no explanation. A younger Bosnian Muslim teacher replaced her. Soon, our class was split: Croat and Serb kids moved to another room, and only the Bosnian Muslim kids stayed behind.

Most of my best friends weren't Muslim. We used to share snacks and jokes. But now, at school, they separated us. At home, their parents wouldn't let them play with us. Our parents said it was just how things are. But later, it all added up: they must have known something was coming.

That's why our new teacher talked so much about mental health—about feelings and behavior. At first, I thought "mental" was a candy! I even started writing down questions to ask him.

Then our school shut down—for good. Mama and Tata said it was for our safety. Safety from who? From what?

Almost no Serbs lived in Žepče. Was some evil war monster waving a Croat flag marching toward us? We didn't believe it—until we did.

Once the War Monster arrived, Mama and Tata began fighting every night and pretending to be best friends by morning. Shelves in shops emptied. Neighbors stopped smiling. Croat and Orthodox Christian friends avoided us.

We Bosniak kids stayed inside, confused and scared.

First came the news. Then silence. Then school segregation. Closures. Bombings. The basement. Tanks. Then barbed wire.

I still don't get it. I thought concentration camp monsters were locked away after World War II. Who let them out? And why?

Next thing I know, we're packing to surrender. Father leaves early. We can't escape. Soldiers patrol everywhere. They know where we live.

Mama and Nana stop crying. Arijana asks me to help pack. She even says "please" and "thank you"—words I never hear from her.

We each pick five outfits, shove them into school backpacks. As we leave the basement, smoke fills the air. The sky is gray like dirty snow. Houses are burning—but not ours. That feels like a small win.

Mama whispers again: "Reason wins over ego." I have no idea what that means. Is it an adult spell or rule? I don't ask—I'm scared she'll scream again. So I stay quiet, nodding as if I understand.

But inside, I'm relieved Tata isn't a bad guy—and thankful our house still stands.

We walk out one by one. We leave our home, our car, everything. We only bring a blanket, some canned food, and the clothes we packed.

Ari spots makeup on the road. "Mom, can I take it? PLEASE?" she pleads, looking up like she's praying. Mother yanks the teddy bear from me: "Hold hands. Don't let go. Say goodbye to your pink bear." I stand frozen, tears welling, Mama avoiding my eyes.

That bruise inside doesn't go away. I'm burning with anger and fear. Everything feels wrong—sounds too loud, smells too strong, the food tastes like metal. My skin hums, my brain spins.

Maybe something's wrong with me. But maybe the whole world is broken.

When did killing neighbors become normal?

I hug Teddy, my chest aching with rage and fear. If I weren't a child, I'd be a bomb. A nuclear explosion.

I kiss Teddy, memorize him, drop him, and we start walking toward barbed wire.

I promise myself not to cry again. I'll do what I'm told. No more smart remarks—where do they think I got it from?

4

Hold Your Horses

Žepče, Bosnia and Herzegovina – June 30, 1993

I am trapped between the backs and breaths of bodies moving around me, feeling invisible and completely alone. It's as if I'm wedged in a sea of shadows with bent spines and panic blooming, quiet but furious. People of all ages dragging their walking dead feet heading to the human cage of silence and screams.

As we are getting closer to the concentration camp, I see not only one—but eight giant tanks. Up until now, I have only seen these giants in movies. They sure look smaller on the screen, I note.

With each resisting step we take toward the barbed-wire hell the concentration camp—Nova Trgovina Camp, located in the warehouse complex of Nova Trgovina company—known in Žepče as Hangari (the hangars)—the atmosphere grows louder and tenser. There are infants, young children, pregnant women, kids my age, teenagers, and elderly people. I drag my two feet as I follow the slow rhythm of the others.

Everywhere I look, people are upset. Some are begging and pleading. Others show no emotion at all. The crowd becomes unbearable to my five senses. My head is throbbing and I feel nauseous. I really have to pee.

I am a big girl. And I'll hold it in, I tell myself. I can't help but notice that since the war began, I'm talking to myself more and more.

"Move your asses and hurry up! Men—to the left. Women, children and elderly to the right," angry Croat soldiers with weapons shout.

"Anything valuable or sharp, dump it in these buckets," a fat soldier with a lazy eye demands.

After my mother takes off her gold wedding band, a pearl necklace and a kitchen knife, and dumps it in a red bucket, another soldier starts going down my mother's body. I am tempted to stand up for her, but my mother shushes me as she puts her index finger on her nose gently.

I get it. She needs me to hold my horses, so I back off. I really want to start hitting, kicking, spitting and cursing at this soldier, but I remind myself, *Aldi, you're only nine.*

This monster has a perverted look in his drunken eyes. His filthy fingers slowly feel every inch of my mother's warm sun-kissed body. I close my big olive eyes just before his fingers touch the sides of her breasts. Mama's wearing a long skirt that goes to her ankles. What if they lift up her dress? I've seen bad guys do such things in movies and each time a scene like that comes up, I take a bathroom break and come back when it's done.

I am not sure what's happening, but it doesn't feel right. I had seen people being searched before on television. This isn't like that. It feels wrong.

"I hate you and I wish you die," I say, covering my lips with my hand. Hoping that he doesn't hear me.

"Aldi, shhhh," my aunt tells me as she grabs my hand and holds it firmly. *Is this wrong and does this make me just as bad as them*, I wonder.

21

The rifle hangs around the soldier's shoulder, and there's a gun in his camouflage army pants. This makes me feel extremely uncomfortable. I squeeze my eyes hard. When I open them—there—I see my father raging, cursing and crying. I can't stand looking at my father like that. My heart wants to jump out of my chest and I feel as if someone is stabbing me over and over, but I can't die.

I don't want my father to feel embarrassed, so I look away for a second. As I turn one last time towards my father, all I see are two Croat soldiers dragging him farther away from us. He glances at the three of us with an apologetic look in his eyes. *It's not your fault, Daddy.*

5

Bathroom

Žepče, Bosnia and Herzegovina – June 30, 1993

Mama searches to find a space for us to settle down. The barracks are too full—no space left to sleep indoors.

"We'll just sleep outside," Mama says as I help her lay a blanket on the concrete ground.

"Outside?" Ari asks, blinking like she didn't hear right.

"I thought you only sleep outside when you're camping," I ask my mother, not realizing that I am breaking my promise to stop asking questions.

"Girls, let's not make a big deal about this," Mama answers with frustration.

"Then, we can go to the bathroom," she adds, like she's offering a reward.

"Finally!" I respond as I bite down my lip. I hate
holding it in.

I remind myself that whenever I suddenly need the bathroom more, it's just my body shouting that I am anxious. I tend to ignore my needs and feelings for as long as I can. I pretend everything is fine even when it isn't. I like to do things my way and at my pace, otherwise I get anxious.

I am afraid if I breathe too loud, they'll shoot us. Ever since the bombing and shooting began, my palms have been dripping with sweat. Ever since we got to the concentration camp, my feet began sweating too. There are no words to describe how I feel. I want to cry, but I can't. My eyes are as sandy as the Sahara.

"The bathroom is behind the barracks," someone in the crowd says.

Me, Ari, and Mama get up and head to the bathroom. There are at least ten people ahead of us waiting.

"Mom, I don't think I can hold it that long," I finally said. I cross my legs and squeeze my muscles as hard as I can.

"You can go in front of us," an older woman wearing a scarf on her head says with pity.

"Hvala vam," Mama says, thanking and holding her hands together, as we skip towards the front of the line. The woman shakes her head downward and smiles.

"Nema na čemu," she answers, letting Mama know it's no biggie.

There are only two people ahead of us. A gentleman in his seventies and his wife around the same age. We are next.

"Mom, where's the toilet and toilet paper," Ari asks.

This girl never stops talking. She hums, makes up stories, asks a million questions that no one wants to answer. Ari thinks Mama can fix everything. She's so dumb, sometimes.

"No toilets. No toilet paper. Just use these tree leaves to wipe yourself," Mama answers as she hands me the green grape leaf to wipe myself.

"Here, you can crouch in this spot. It's still dry," she points with her index finger.

I'm embarrassed to pull down my pants in front of others. There's an older man and his wife across from us. "Mama, what if they see me?"

"Nobody is going to see you. I'll guard you," she says standing beside me like a shield.

"Thank you, mama," I smile at her. Peeing hurts like never before, but I do it anyway.

After the three of us are done, we leave. As we sit down, Ari questions, "Mama, when do we go home?"

"Soon. Now, sit and play with your sister quietly,"

Mama answers.

6

Bread and Stars

Žepče, Bosnia and Herzegovina – July 1, 1993

Arijana picks up a pebble and starts scratching little shapes into the dirt—bread, stars, hearts and suns.

"Let me show you how to draw a house. Our house, with beds, toilet and showers." I even draw Mama, Tata, Ari and myself all waving with smiles on our faces.

"I wish we were there," Ari says, her voice quieter now.

"Me too!" I whisper into her ear as I press my lips on her cheek.

The day is warm, but as night approaches the temperature drops. My stomach gurgles and I'm thirsty. Mama gives us a sip of water from a liter canister and a piece of store-bought toast that we eat in silence.

The night scares me, but tonight's fear is different. Bigger. Heavier. The silver lantern of the moon and the tiny star-lights sprinkle the darkness like glitter on the ground. I find myself zoning out into the sky. Every time I do this, I pick a different star to stare at. I make a game out of it.

I count in my head—*Thirty...Sixty...Ninety...*

My record is hundred and twenty seconds—that's two minutes of being checked out. This makes me feel victorious. It makes my brain hurt less. If I can't physically escape this place where time is buried—then I'll escape this way. With my eyes. My brain bosses my eyes, forces them to stay locked on the star, to stay in the nothingness. But my eyes fight back. They protest with tears. They blink and blur. And I start again.

Whenever Mama looks at me, I close my eyes and I pretend I'm asleep. Each time I hear a movement, a cry and a scream, I stick my wounded index fingers into my two ears. It doesn't block the sound completely but makes them feel farther away—like they are happening to someone else. At some point, toward dawn, my eyes give up on me and I finally fall asleep. But it's never for long. I wake up gasping—like I'm drowning. The nightmare is still under my ribs, pressing against my chest. I don't remember what I dreamed.

I wake up staring at an open sky that looks like a child colored it with crayons—yellow, peach and a little bit of pink. Women whisper nearby, their voices mixing with the proud cries of roosters doing their job. My eyes are dry and itchy. The stars are gone, but the moon still hangs there. Its crescent shape reminds me of a croissant. I'm so hungry. If I could, I'd eat a dozen croissants all by myself.

Last night, some women and beautiful young girls were taken. Everyone knows, but no one talks about it out loud.

"Where do they take the pretty girls?" I ask my mother.

"Aldi. You're only nine," she says, then pauses to think. "Too young to understand," she sighs, brushing dust off her skin. "Now, come on. Let's go stand in line for food."

"Fine!" I say with a huff, crossing my arms. I don't get it. *Suddenly, I'm too young to understand. But if I'm so young, why don't Mama and Tata hold me anymore? Why do they only pick up Ari? Why am I the one telling her stories, getting yelled at, pretending I'm not scared? Why do I have to be the strong one—the one who holds back her tears? This is bullshit. Nobody said, "You're young—so you get to keep your pink teddy bear." No. That got taken too.*

Sometimes I imagine we're American. My parents would call me "sweetie," not "sine," like I'm their son instead of their daughter. If I was American, I wouldn't be leaving my home, my life, and going to some stupid concentration camp. If I was American, the worst punishment I'd get would be no dessert after dinner. Not motka. Not standing in the corner with my nose to the wall until they decided I'd had enough. Mama and Tata would say "Could you please" and "thank you" instead of "odmah," do it now, or "začepi," shut up.

Sometimes I even wish Mama and Tata weren't my real parents. Maybe my *real* parents would actually like me more than Ari. Maybe they'd never yell at me or hit me or make me stand in a corner. Maybe they'd buy me ice cream every day and let me keep my teddy bear and not care if I cried.

Deep down, I'm scared to know. I can tell Mama is afraid and uncomfortable. She hides it with her voice, but I can tell in her eyes. Eyes never lie. I can tell, she doesn't want me to ask questions—especially not that kind. Next time I want to know something, I'll ask one of my aunts. Maybe, they'll tell me the truth.

Ever since the war began, the adults have been keeping secrets. They lie. A lot. And it's not fair—because when we lie, we get in trouble.

7

I'm Glad I'm Not Pretty

Žepče, Bosnia and Herzegovina – July 1, 1993

It's time to line up. The three of us go wait for food. The line is so long. I shift from foot to foot, trying not to think about how slow it's moving. My stomach growls loudly and I imagine breakfast: eggs, cheese, smoked beef, and tomatoes. I picture the table we used to sit around, the smell of fresh homemade bread, Mama pouring chamomile. I hope they feed us well today. We barely ate anything yesterday. The line creeps forward. My stomach feels weird and sour. The acid is so strong, I swear I can smell it. It stings the back of my throat. I try not to cry, but my eyes are hot.

"Is it our turn, yet?" Ari asks for the millionth time as tears roll down her pink cheeks.

"Shhh, sweetheart! Please don't cry—we're almost there," Mama says with a sigh, telling another white lie.

"I'm really hungry," Ari sniffles, wiping her honey-colored eyes with the back of her hand.

I stay quiet. I don't complain about my hunger, even though my stomach twists and aches. That's how I'll help Mama—by not making things worse. After what feels like forever, it's finally our turn. But there are no eggs. No cheese. No smoked meat. No croissants. No tomatoes. Just a piece of stale bread, a teaspoon of forest fruit jam, and a small cup of water. We take our meal and return to our blanket.

"Ouch! My tooth!" Ari winces, covering her cheek with her palm.

"Arijana—can't you stop complaining for once?" Mama snaps, her voice sharp with exhaustion as she shoots her the dirty look. Then, she softens.

"This might be our only meal today. Let me sprinkle a little water on the bread."

She wets the crust with trembling fingers and slowly spreads the jam across it, handing the softened piece to my sister like it's treasure.

I eat. With each bite, I plug my nose and chew the dry bread over and over, until it's soft enough to swallow. I used to love jam. But this one tastes off—metallic and salty like a tin it came from or like someone cried into the jar. I finish it as fast as I can.

My aunts are working in the kitchen. We're hoping they can sneak an extra piece of bread every now and then–take turns giving it to one of us. Maybe tomorrow, it will be my turn?

I am bored out of my mind. I wish I had a book to read, but there are no books here. I want to keep a journal, but I wasn't allowed to bring one. Even if I did have something to write in, Mama would probably say it's too dangerous. I wish I could color. Or play with my friends. But that's dangerous too.

All of my friends are here somewhere, with their mothers, aunts or grandmothers. But we don't see each other. We are not allowed to walk around the concentration camp—unless we're going to get food or going to the "bathroom."

"Don't bring attention to yourselves," she always says. So, we don't. We shrink. We wait.

I hate being still. I hate being quiet. I'm so tired of all this crap.

"Aldijana, how many times do I have to tell you—take your fingers out of your mouth!" Mama snaps, again. "Look what you've done to yourself!" she mutters, pulling a white handkerchief from her pocket and wrapping it tightly around my left ring finger.

I don't answer. I don't even look at her. Sometimes, she's just so annoying.

It's humid and my skin feels sticky and gross. I sneak a sniff of my armpits and hope no one sees me. I don't want people thinking I'm weird. It's bad enough I'm dressed in these baggy clothes that make me look like a boy.

It's almost nighttime again. I wonder if the drunk soldiers will take more pretty girls tonight. I don't understand why they only come at night. Or why they only take pretty ones. Maybe they make them cook and clean and do laundry? Maybe they treat them like maids? I hope so. I hope it's just that.

I'm glad I am not pretty. My hair is short and messy. I run my fingers through it to make sure. I touch my chest to check—still flat. Good. I could still pass as a boy.

The drunk soldiers never take boys. In Berek, there are more boys than girls–and all the girls are either too old or too young—so I grew up a tomboy.

Before the real war began, one of our favorite games was playing war. It's almost as if we called it into being. Some of us were the good guys, and others were the bad guys. Since I was the only girl, they didn't think I had it in me to be the bad guy. But they were wrong. Anyone can be good or bad–it just depends on what you pick. Look what they picked.

Whenever we played 'war' before the war, we played the good guys and always got ambushed when we least expected. The bad guys threw rocks at us. They stole our supplies. They kidnapped our people, they made their own bows and arrows.

My twelve-year-old cousin Ado, who lives next door, and is only a few years older than me, was their leader. He's the closest thing I've had to an annoying brother. Ado's stare—with his washed–out blue eyes—could make me cry without saying a word. His dad is Tata's brother—, my uncle, Nurija. Tata also has four sisters—my aunts—Tetka Advija, Tetka Azra, Tetka Besima and Tetka Fatima.

Ado and I never saw eye to eye. He loved yanking my curls, pulling down my pants, stealing my snacks, making me cry—then laughing in my face. Last New Year's Eve—after the grown-ups fired a handgun into the sky to welcome the new year–Ado and I raced downstairs to see who could find the shell casing first. The next thing I remember is my father's calloused hand on my cheek... and an ocean of tears running down it. For the longest time, I hated them both because of what happened this night. Ado stealing the shell casing from me. Tata punishing me. But now that we're all trapped in here, packed together like ghosts still pretending to be alive–I'd give anything to free them. Yesterday I saw Ado. He handed me half of his bread, no questions asked. That wasn't like him. It's almost like he grew up overnight.

8

Santa Doesn't Jump Barbed Wires

Žepče, Bosnia and Herzegovina – July 2, 1993

A t Hangari, we don't sleep in real beds. We don't have a roof over our heads. We don't get real bathrooms. We don't get seconds; we definitely don't get extras. Just thinking about food makes my stomach growl—again.

Mama was wrong this morning—we are getting a second meal. It's dinner time and, once again, we wait in line. But our line isn't moving. We are stuck. There's a burning sensation in my calves, and I want to sit down and eat. But of course, I'm not allowed. If you want to eat, you have to stand—no matter how tired, sick or old you are. There are no exceptions.

Arijana keeps whining. Mama shushes her and lifts her up every now and then to calm her down. I wish she would lift me up and hold me.

The line starts to crawl forward. My eyes land at a girl from school—she's maybe eleven, with thick blond hair falling all the way down her back. It's messy, but still pretty.

I reach for my own head—my curls feel like a bird's nest. I hate my hair. It reminds me of Ado. Mama says I got it from my father. He used to have curls, too.

"For God's sake, cut that girl's hair before they hurt her, "Mama says.

I don't get it. I'd kill to have hair like that—Mama knew it was better to hide pretty in here.

Tonight's dinner is watered down bean soup, a piece of cornbread that smells weird. I extend my arm, holding out my plastic bowl. Aunt Fatima is serving. She winks at me and blows a kiss. I kiss my right hand and blow her back an even bigger one. I don't get extra food—but her kiss and her wink make my day. We take our food back to our blanket in the hangars. We eat, then we stay in our small corner full of tired, quiet faces.

We're not allowed to do anything, so I watch people. I imagine who they were before all of this. Some faces look familiar—close and distant family, classmates and friends. My eyes land on my two cousins. I want to run to them with open arms and hug them. I want to tell Ado that I forgive him. But I don't. Because I know, that's not allowed.

Instead, I lay down. I'm not sleepy. I hear babies crying. Old people coughing. Farting. Mothers whispering, trying to shush their kids.

Being indoors feels somewhat safer than being outside. Croat soldiers patrol with rifles slung over their shoulders and guns always within reach. As long as I stay quiet and don't draw attention, we'll be fine.

Ari loves when I tell stories. She never gets tired of them. So, I tell her the one about the day we first met.

"Father went to Zenica to pick you and Mom up. I stayed home with Nana Điha, waiting for you. At first, I didn't understand why everyone made such a big deal about being a big sister. But then, I saw you—your big honey-colored eyes and chubby cheeks. You looked like a doll. I wanted to hold you all the time and play with you. Mom of course was super careful whenever she let me. Up until that day, I had never asked the neighbors if I could pick flowers from their garden. But that day, I did. I wanted to show that I was responsible enough to be a big sister. I didn't want the first thing you heard about me to be that I was a flower thief. Ari, the day you were born, I decided I didn't want to be just a troublemaker. I reinvented myself. I graduated from the School of Troublemakers. And you—you became the new troublemaker in our family. I won't let the Croats, Serbs or any other soldiers hurt you. I am your big sister. It's my job to keep you safe," I say looking at her baby face.

"Aldi, what are you two talking about?" Mama asks curiously.

"Nothing, Mom," I answer, realizing that I should stop being everybody's mom. Aldi, you're only nine—I remind myself.

"I know," Ari mumbles through a yawn, rubbing her tired eyes. Before I'm able to continue my story, she's already asleep. So, I think back to the time Tata dressed up as Santa for New Year's Eve.

Santa didn't visit all Bosniak kids—just the ones with fathers like mine. Fathers who drank rakija. Fathers who didn't pray. Fathers who skipped mosque but still called themselves good people. Fathers who let their kids decorate trees and believe in magic. Santa never showed up to homes where kids called their dads Babo. Only the ones who said Tata—like the Croats and Serbs. Fathers like mine.

I can't seem to find a comfortable spot. Even though I'm exhausted, I can't fall asleep. So, I think back to the time Tata dressed up as Santa for New Year's Eve.

We didn't get Santa on Christmas, because Muslims don't celebrate Christmas. We got Santa on New Year's Eve. He wore a red suit, had rosy cheeks, a white beard, big glasses, and a booming laugh.

We celebrated New Year's just after Christmas. We decorated our tree and exchanged gifts like everyone else. Along with the two Muslim religious Eid holidays, New Year's Eve was my favorite holiday.

On Eid mornings, we'd hug and kiss our parents, grandparents, aunts, uncles, and neighbors. Then we'd stuff our wallets with money and head out in big groups.

"Our religion celebrates two major holidays," Nana Điha used to explain to our Catholic and Christian neighbors.

The first is Eid al-Fitr, marking the end of Ramadan, the month of fasting and charity. On that day, our tables overflowed with sarma, burek, sirnica, lukovice, somun, begova čorba, bosanski lonac, and punjene paprike—dishes so rich and flavorful you could gain back all the weight you lost during Ramadan in just one day.

For dessert: baklava, hurmašice, šampita, rolat, oblatna, halva, kadaif. The scents alone were intoxicating. After morning prayers, families gathered to eat, laugh, share stories, pray, listen to sevdah, traditional music, and dance the kolo, circle dance. It was beautiful. Joyful. Sacred. And on New Year's Day—we got presents.

Some Catholic and Orthodox kids from the neighborhood joined in our Eid celebrations, too. Who wouldn't when there was money involved? And just like that, some of their kids got to enjoy our Muslim holiday rituals too. Not all Serb and Croat families allowed it, but some did. They let their children come with us, knock on doors, say the greetings, and share the joy.

Out of mutual respect, we joined in their celebrations as well. On Eid, all you had to do was say, "Bajram Šerif Mubarek Olsun!" or Eid Mubarak, and kiss the hand of the person who opened the door. Most of us didn't mind doing that. We only kissed the hands of our relatives—who smiled and gave us money.

The second Eid, Eid al-Adha—or Kurban Bajram—came after Hajj, the pilgrimage to Mecca. Those who could afford it would sacrifice a lamb or cow and share the meat with family, friends, and neighbors. It was celebrated the same way: food, laughter, music, prayer, and joy.

On Easter, we colored eggs. On the Day of the Dead, we jumped over bonfires with our Croatian friends.

Before the war, it didn't matter what religion you followed. We lived by values of unity, respect, and love. We believed in one God. We believed in being good, moral, decent people. That was all that mattered.

I remember the excitement I felt when Santa Claus knocked. I remember the joy. But Santa doesn't visit concentration camps.

9

When Mama Dreams

Žepče, Bosnia and Herzegovina – July 2, 1993

I wonder what time it is, but we don't have clocks or watches. My eyes sting from lack of sleep, but I force myself to stay awake, listening to the whispers around us. Mama is talking quietly with her sister, Tetka Majda. Someone shushes them, reminding everyone to get some sleep. Anela, my three-year-old cousin, has been asleep for a long time. Her father, Uncle Hamza is somewhere out there defending Bosniaks.

"Senada, we'll talk tomorrow," Aunt Majda says as she wraps her arms around Anela.

Mama nods and lays down on the concrete floor next to Ari, who's in the middle of us. She keeps tossing and turning. She looks uncomfortable. Nervous. She's barely smoked since we got here. If she has, she's hidden it. I haven't seen her holding a cigarette in between her pointer and middle fingers. The other night, after I woke up to go to the bathroom, I saw her hand resting between her face—those two fingers in a v-shape, like she was dreaming about smoking.

I wonder if she'll get any sleep tonight. Mama has always struggled with sleep—even before war. And now that we are in this prison, it's even worse.

Every time I look at her, her fingers are tracing the patterns of our blanket or she's staring at the ceiling.

Since they locked us in here, her eyes have stayed puffy. Her face looks grayer than usual. She looks pale as she hasn't seen the sun in weeks. The brown bags under her eyes have deepened. Each morning she wakes up looking older. Thinner. But Mama still has the most beautiful smile. And those dimples—those are mine too.

Her parents, my grandparents from Maglaj, are also here, imprisoned in Nova Trgovina Camp, along with her two brothers, Uncle Nurija and Uncle Senad, their wives and their children. My father's sister from Maglaj, Aunt Advija, and Uncle Esad–who had a stroke the very first day the war began in Maglaj–are here too.

Maglaj was hit before Žepče, so both my maternal and paternal families have been refugees in Žepče for quite a while.

When Žepče fell, and we had no choice but to turn ourselves in, our family from Maglaj did the same. Like my father, my uncles were taken to another concentration camp location, and we don't know if any of them are alive. Some nights, I close my eyes and try to picture my male relatives–their warm laughs and the sound of their voices. Sometimes, I try to count how many of us are here, but I always forget someone.

The air tastes like cold concrete and old fear. I cover my head with our big brown blanket with faded flower patterns. I lay on my right side. My body aches and even though there's a blanket underneath us, the floor is ice cold. I wrap my left arm around Ari's six-year-old body to warm up. At some point towards the morning, I fall asleep. Mama stays awake.

10

Don't Look

Žepče, Bosnia and Herzegovina – Early July 1993

A minute here feels like a day outside, so I stop counting days. It's not worth it. Our routines here are the same every day, but the moods and egos of the soldiers aren't.

"Ego is pride," my aunt, Tetka Fatima, finally explains.

Some days, the Croat soldiers are more aggressive and rude. Other days, they are more quiet because they are hung over. On these hungover days, they are also more irritable, so we try to be quieter. We never know what's going to trigger them and make them snap. I feel like we are walking on eggshells and needles and we never know when one of them will explode.

We are only allowed to move around to get food or to go behind the barracks to relieve ourselves. Everything else is forbidden. Every time I ask "could we"–the answer is always no.

It's been days since we last showered. I can't stand the smell. It's like no other smell before. I can't really describe it. It's very uncomfortable. Anytime someone opens their mouth and begins speaking, I take a step back. Standing in line for food and bathroom requires a lot of mouth breathing and nose pinching. I'm getting good at it.

I imagine taking a bath in my own home and sleeping in my bunk bed. Before the war, I hated brushing my teeth. If the war ever stops, I promise to brush them three times a day.

The mustiness becomes overwhelming for everyone including our captors, so they let us wash up. Finally, we get to go down to the River Bosna and cleanse our sweaty bodies. I absolutely love water. There's something so relaxing and peaceful about it.

Summertime in Žepče is my favorite time of the year.

My birthday is in May, school ends in June and then we're on break. Every summer we go down to the river and swim. My boy cousins are daredevils and they all dive. This year was the year when I was supposed to learn to dive–and not worry whether or not I'll die.

The group of soldiers walk us outside the gated concentration camp. Each family gets a bar of soap and a towel. Bosna is just down the gate. The sun is out and it's very humid. I can't wait to feel the water on my skin. I can't wait to smell the river and have the soap wash away my funky body and oily hair.

"What about our bathing suits?" Ari points out.

"Who needs bathing suits when you can stay in your shorts and tank top," Mama tries to make this exciting.

"You're right, Mom!" I add as I wink at her. Then I whisper into my mother's ear, so Arijana can't hear, "as long as they don't ask us to take our clothes off. Are they?"

"They won't do that," she whispers back. I pretend I believe her and I smile.

Pretty soon, we're by the river. People who live in Preko, on the other side of the Bosnian River—Rjeka Bosna —are so lucky not to be imprisoned like us. Most of them have escaped to Bosniak controlled villages and Zenica. There's a rumor that my aunt Azra and her kids are in Vranduk at Tetka Besima's. I wish I was in Vranduk too.

As we enter the cold water of Rjeka Bosna in our outfits, with their big and heavy rifles and their loud perverted laugh—we are reminded that this isn't a fun day at the beach.

The water is brownish even though it hasn't rained since we got to concentration camp. Because it's too hot outside, my body struggles to adjust to the cold Bosna. We only go as far as our hips. With my two hands I scoop water and wet myself all over. Then, I dunk myself into it. It's still cold, but not as much. Mama rubs weird-smelling soap all over Ari. I wait for my turn at the soap. I scooch my body down to avoid being watched. I plug my ears and I wait. Soon, Mama passes me the soap. I try to grab it, but it slips down my hand. Before it touches the ground, Mama catches it.

"Be careful!" she warns me.

"Okay, Mom!" I answer her feeling uneasy. This time, I make sure that I grab onto the soap and that it stays in my shaky hands. It has no smell to it and I feel as if I'm washing my body with a rock. First, I scrub my hair. Next, I pick up my sleeves and wash my armpits. Then, I raise my t-shirt and wash under it. I pause.

I could hear my heart pounding. There's this heaviness in between my breasts as if I'm getting stabbed. I move my head to the right–then to the left—as I quickly cleanse under my underwear–making sure they don't see me.

I pass the soap to Mama and I grab onto Arijana's hand. "Let's play who can hold their breath the longest underwater," I tell my sister.

"Yaaaay! I'm gonna win!" she utters with excitement.

"No, you're not! I'm gonna beat you!" I answer competitively as I stick my tongue out—wanting to beat her and show her who's the boss. If I do beat her, she'll cry like a crybaby as she is–and then—I'll get in trouble.

"Mama, she's making fun of me! Tell her to stop," Ari whines and tattles on me, like she always does.

"Aldi, enough! Pamet u glavu," a phrase I hate hearing—mind in the head—as if I already don't have a brain in my head.

"But Mom–she's such a tattle tale!

"Ignore her. She's still little," she points out.

I can't help but feel Arijana is her favorite. And I'm not? "It's not fair!" I respond as I cross my arms.

It's not worth it. I'll let Ari win. Maybe, just once, I should take one for the team. With one hand, my "little sister" and I plug our noses as neither one knows how to hold our breath under water.

"One…two…three…GO!" simultaneously we shout as we squeeze each other's fingers and go in until our heads are no longer visible.

Seconds later, after most of the soap comes off my skin, I stick my head out. Arijana's head comes after.

"I WON! I WON! I WON!'" she continues to brag as if she's won the lottery and not some stupid game that I let her win.

I turn towards Mama and see her index finger pointing up and touching the middle of her nose. My eyes stare at my mother's nonexistent nails. At least, I have some.

"Shhhhhhhh!" with her raised eyebrows she scolds us. Then she moves her index finger left to right.

"FINE! We'll be quiet," we both answer with sass.

All of the sudden, we hear, "Help! Help! Help" and the very loud cynical laugh of the Croat soldiers.

"Look over there!" someone shouts as we all move our heads towards the middle of River Bosna.

"Mama! It's a DEAD BODY!" Arijana and I scream trying to beat each other at who's gonna get Mama's attention first. The soap from Mom's hand drops and she freezes.

This time I won. I wasn't going to let Arijana beat me twice.

"Mama, pick me up and hold me!" Arijana cries.

"Girls, don't look! Look at my face and do what I do. Take a deep breath and hold it in—hold it in. Keep holding it in—then blow it out," she tells us as she gently moves our cheeks away from the dead man's body—but it's too late.

"Mama, pick me up and hold me!" Arijana repeats over and over until Mama hears her out.

Mama takes my hand and pulls on it. I try to move my legs, but my legs are refusing to listen. I am paralyzed. Tears are falling down my cheeks and I can't swallow my saliva. There's a lump in my throat and I'm suffocating. My heart is loud and I feel it's about to jump out of my chest.

"Aldi, let's go! We gotta move. NOW!" Mama screams.

My legs continue to feel as if I'm standing in quicksand. I'm trying to move them, but I can't. My eyes are glued on the dead corpse.

"Am I dreaming?" I hear my voice and realize that I'm talking to myself, again.

11

Scavengers

Žepče, Bosnia and Herzegovina – Early July 1993

The bloated, greenish-black body floats in River Bosna—burned into my brain, on replay. The dead man—again and again and again.

A black leather jacket and cargo pants indicate that he was a civilian—not a soldier.

Scavengers—black ravens munching on what's left over from the decomposing face, neck, back, arms, abdomen, legs and feet. His eyes maggot infested, and his nose cartilage exposed. His skin separating from the tissue and his boney knee popping through the ripped pants. That awful gassy odor.

This isn't happening! Wake up! I tell myself as I pinch my cheeks, and soon after, realize that this isn't a nightmare.

"Mom, wait for me!" I shout after noticing that Mama let go of my hand.

"Mama, wait for me!" I cry even louder as I race out of the water, afraid that they'll leave me behind with the dead man and the scavengers.

"I got you, baby," Mama says the nicest thing to me since the war began as she holds me in her lap and rocks me back and forth until my body no longer feels the panic.

12

The Exchange List

Žepče, Bosnia and Herzegovina – Early July 1993

Everyone's been on the edge since we got here and it's only getting worse. We've been imprisoned for seven days. Mama hasn't slept, eaten or smoked–and she loves her cigarettes. Ari and I bicker and get on each other's nerves, more and more. I don't know how much longer, before someone snaps. I miss home. I miss my life before this havoc. I think about my Tata and I wonder if he's okay. Each night I wake up with ice crawling down my neck, gasping for air in the dark.

Sometimes, it's the sound of my own high-pitched panicked cry that wakes me. I look around and can hear my veins thudding, pumping blood to my heart like a drumbeat.

Mother says that he's alive. She just knows—feels it in her gut. What's gut got to do with knowing things? If she's wrong about the war ending soon—maybe she's wrong about Father too. What if I forget his voice? Or the way he looks?

Lately, Mama just sits with her arms wrapped around her knees. She rocks a little, like she's trying to keep something inside from breaking loose. Before the war, Father used to whistle in the mornings while brushing his teeth. Every day after work, he went down to the basement to build wooden chairs, tables, doors and windows. Carpentry was his true passion.

One time, Mama sent me downstairs to call him to come up to eat. The radio was playing Sevdah music and my father followed along—lyric by lyric. Even his voice sounded melodic. He made up little songs with our names in them. I can still hear the way he stretched out the vowels—Aaal-dee-yah-nah and—Aah-ree-yah-nah—just to make the two of us laugh.

I've been forgetting things. Things I never should. Our Eids. Ramadan Iftars, the meal that ends our daily fast during Eids. I try to remember the smell of Mama's baklava fresh out of the oven. I can't remember the taste of anything anymore. My heart craves hearing the melodic adhan—the voice in Arabic that echoes five times a day to announce daily prayer and walking to the mosque with Grandmother Điha and Zulka.

It's like all the good memories are fogged over—little by little—drowning in the ocean of the war's ugliness.

My chest tightens. My stomach feels hollow. I want to scream, but nothing comes out. If I forget who we were, how will I know who I am? If I forget the good, how can I be good?

Just when I feel like the past is slipping away, Mama gets a letter that was smuggled in through a neighbor. The three of us gather into a circle. Mama opens the envelope carefully—like this is the most valuable thing she ever had. Her fingers tremble. She has no nails anymore, only crusted edges, a thin line of what used to be.

Dear Senada, Aldi and Ari,

I hope this letter finds you safe. I don't know where you are exactly, but not a moment passes without me thinking of you. I ask God every day to watch over you, to give you strength, and to bring us back together. Aldijana, take care of your sister. I know how brave you are, and I trust you are helping Mama in every way you can. Arijana, I hope you are still asking your endless questions and singing those silly songs. I can still hear your voice in my mind.

Senada, the three of you mean the world to me. One of the prisoners says that the civilians may be allowed to get out. He overheard the soldiers holding us imprisoned. Tomorrow–add your names to the Exchange List. You'll be picked to leave. Trust me. Just do it. Leave now. Azra, Fatima and their kids are in Vranduk at Asim and Besima's place. Go there. Don't look back. And don't worry about me. I am alive. I am safe—for now. That is all I can say in this letter. I don't know when I'll be able to write again, but I will try. Hold on. Keep believing. Remember who you are. Remember our home. We will see each other again. We must.

With all my heart,

Your love

13

Words I'm Afraid to Ask

Žepče, Bosnia and Herzegovina – Early July 1993

Mama holds the letter in her shaky hands. She reads the first sentence. Then—she stops. A sea of tears spill down her face. Her voice cracks. Her lips move, but no sound comes out. She covers her face trying to hide. Turns her head to the side. Mucus slips from her nostrils. Nana Zulka—her mom—wipes it gently, the way she used to when Mama was little. At that moment—my mother isn't a wife. She isn't a mother. She is Senada—a child in a grown-up's body.

Arijana and I wrap our arms around her, trying to make the crying stop. Majka Zulka opens her wide shoulders and pulls us all in—her big elbows folding around the three of us like wings. Dido Hašim who was standing like a statue, lowers himself to the floor. He kneels, resting his hands on his bent knees. Tears roll from his dark brown eyes, soaking into his black mustache and the beard he's stopped trimming.

Nana Điha's hands are parallel to her blue eyes—the same eyes Tata has. Her lips move. She's making a dua—praying. Then, she recites El-Fatiha, her voice steady and strong. She ends her prayer with Amin. I don't say anything. I just listen.

49

For a second, the war disappears. The hunger in my belly doesn't matter. The knot in my throat disappears. It's just us. A family holding onto each other like an umbrella in the rain.

Mama folds the letter and puts it back into an envelope. Her hands are still shaking, but slower now, like they're tired from dancing. Her face is dry–but the rash and puffiness on her high cheekbones—like proof that she broke for a moment. That was then. Now, she's back. It's like she has hardened. Like she grew balls.

"We have to go," she says, her voice hoarse. No one moves. "We have to add our names to the Exchange List. my love said to trust him."

Nana takes off her thick glasses and wipes them down with her dimije, a long traditional skirt with lots of patterns. She sighs the longest sigh then smiles sarcastically. "Your love knows the best. We'll follow you." Mama gives her a stare.

Mama says nothing, but her look is enough to tell that Nana needs to stay out of it.

"But what if it's a trap?" Dido Hašim asks, combing his mustache to calm down his nerves.

Mama doesn't answer right away. She pulls the quarter of a cigarette from her bra and lights it with a

cheap lighter. The soldiers aren't nearby. She takes a long puff, like the nicotine might fix something broken. Then, she passes the cigarette to Nana Điha. Next, it travels to Dido Hašim. I don't get why cigarettes are named after beautiful rivers. He holds it in between his fingers the longest. Then–Majka, who I have never seen smoke snitches it right out of his hand. The one scarred with old burns he gave himself crafting horseshoes for living.

"What the hell is wrong with them all?" I whisper to Ari.

She looks down at the ground and moves her shoulders up letting me know that she's as clueless as me.

"It's a risk we must take," Mama answers like she's putting a period at the end of a sentence.

"Staying here, might be worse. What if we starve? Get sick? Die? And God forbid get raped?" Her voice slices the air, sharp and raw like she's bleeding somewhere nobody can see.

"Hey. Hey. Hey. Slow down, now–SENADA." Dido Hašim raises his voice at his grown daughter. That's not like him. Yelling is Majka Zulka's thing. She's the one that nags and complains. But not him. He never yells. He's the one that always says yes. The one who hands us cash every time he sees, like there's no tomorrow.

War changes people. It makes them do things they'd never done before. It's changing me too. I don't feel like a little kid anymore. It's almost as If I grew up overnight. Before the war I watched Tom and Jerry, the Smurfs, and read fairy tales. Now I watch people come apart. I hear words like rape—and that word gives me goosebumps.

I don't know exactly what rape is, but I'm afraid to ask. It sounds worse than dying. I keep thinking about the pretty girls the soldiers take at night. Only a few days ago, I thought they were maids. Now I think they are something worse.

Mama looks down. Cigarette is back in her hand. She's got the face that says sharing time is over. Her cheeks flush red, just like the lipstick she used to wear. If she could take the words back, she would. But it's too late now. Thank God, Arijana was playing with her imaginary friends. She didn't hear it.

"Watch the kids for me? Mama says, "I'll be right back."

"I'm in charge now. And I'm choosing to give my daughters a chance. For God's sake, they're only children."

14

Scratch Marks

Žepče, Bosnia and Herzegovina – Early July 1993

Last night, my eyes stayed wide open. It's almost as if Mama's insomnia spread onto me. My body itches in front of this new disease. I stay up the whole night taking it out on my skin as if this war is my skin's fault. My skin has already changed. How many more times will it change? I hate not knowing myself. I hate not knowing what the exchange will bring. What if we're tricked? What then? At least here—we have a routine. And we're alive. For now.

Mother already packs our rucksacks. After our names get picked, she runs home. The Croat soldiers with big guns watch her closely, they follow her home. When she comes back, her face is pale. She brings clean clothes, our papers, and one small photo album. Her hands tremble as she zips the bag. I see her slip some money into her bra—the only place the soldiers haven't searched. Not yet. Her eyes meet mine, and I know she's scared too. When she isn't tossing and turning, she's going to the bathroom. She's either on one of her lady days or about to crap her pants. I make sure she doesn't see the bruises on my skin—from angry scratching. If she does, she'd think the Croats have done to me what they do to pretty girls.

Arijana snores. At some point in the night, she gets up. Her eyes are closed. She mumbles something through her teeth. Both arms move like they're trying to navigate. I look for Mama. She must be in the "bathroom." The rest of the family members all seem asleep.

"Ari...Ari...Arijana. Open your eyes! Look at me," I whisper, trying not to wake anyone up.

Arijana doesn't respond. She ignores me. Like always. Says that I need to stop bossing her around.

"Aaaa-rhee-yaaaah-naaaah! WAKE UP! NOW," I no longer whisper. My hands are shaking. And I'm shaking her.

"Aldi–STOP. Leave her alone!" Mama's voice suddenly appears and stops me before I cause more damage.

"I hate you. And I'm sick and tired of you ignoring me and giving her all the attention!" I shout as loudly as I can, as If this will make things better.

It doesn't. It only makes it worse. I feel like a piece of shit. I don't hate her. Or my sister. Or my dad. If anything–I'm angry. Ever since Arijana was born, my mom and dad haven't looked at me the same way. Everything's always about her.

"I'm so tired of this bullshit! Ground me forever—if you want. Spank me. Like I care. It won't hurt. It never does."

"Are you guys out of your mind? Do you want to get killed before you even try to escape?" Dido Hašim gets the last word, as he should.

Mama doesn't scold me. She looks at me in a way that she's never looked at me before. Admiring me.

What the heck? If there's one positive change that came out of this war—it's Mama—suddenly okay with me being a smartass.

15

The Lucky Ones

Žepče, Bosnia and Herzegovina – Early July 1993

I t's time to leave. It's time to leave. I heard the adults whispering that the three of us have to go before the rest of the family because of Tata's work in the military and how important he was before the war. Tata was *vojno lice*, which means he had some big job in the army before everything fell apart.

Nana Điha said Tata could have saved himself. He could have swum across the river Bosna like many men did to escape. But he didn't. He turned himself in because of us. He was afraid the three of us would be easy targets. We're just women, and we're the family of a Bosniak, a Muslim military official who still calls himself a Yugoslav and believes in *bratstvo i jedinstvo*, brotherhood and unity. Like in the old days when everyone was supposed to be friends no matter what they believed.

The three of us are on the first exchange list. *I wonder why. How did Tata do that? Did he pay someone? Did he bribe someone? I don't know. Maybe it's because we're his family. Or maybe it's because they think we're not strong enough to survive here.*

I don't understand why he didn't swim and then come get us later. Or why we can't all just swim together. I know how to swim. Ari doesn't, but she could ride on his back like when we play in the river. Maybe they don't want to get wet?

Nana Điha doesn't cry. Not this time. Neither does Majka Zulka, but she never does. Dido Hašim says he has a stomach flu, so he's not coming to see us off. I think he's lying. Maybe goodbyes make his stomach hurt. He doesn't say goodbye.

I wish they were coming with us. But it was just the three of us. We were the lucky ones.

My aunt Strina Ševala, Edo and Ado kick the newspaper roll back and forth–like they used to kick a soccer ball. My aunt waves and she blows us a kiss. A boy taller than my two cousins seemingly older too, wears a skirt and a blouse, his face flushing with embarrassment. Edo trips Ado who's seemingly upset. Ado touches the corners of his ears with his thumbs, looking like an elk. Then, he sticks his tongue out at me. Strina sees this, and she slaps his right hand with one of her own. I feel sorry for Strina.

Tetka Advija and her eighteen-year-old daughter are pulling down my uncle Tetak Esad's trousers and putting what seems to be a diaper on him. I look away, feeling uncomfortable. Esad lifts up his cane and waves it at us. Tetka Advija avoids eye contact. I know she's hiding her tears. Their only daughter looks up with her beautiful hazel eyes and she smiles. Then she makes a heart with her hands—one for me—one for Ari. I fold my arms and I make an even bigger heart.

Majka braids my cousin's long black hair. Another cousin has a stick in his hands, moves it back and forth and making noise with his mouth—like he's playing with a real toy car. My aunt who's running after my cousin and stops to wave a goodbye. Nana is holding my baby cousin—the two of them are clapping and singing.

Part of me can't wait to get the hell out of this shithole. The other part wants to stay. It's almost as if I was getting used to being imprisoned. Mama's in a rush. She walks as if she's running on needles. Nobody cries.

We turn one last time. I count my family members. Using my finger, like I'm pressing one of the buttons on my camera to take one last picture of them.

One. Two. Three. Four. Five. Six. Seven. Eight. Nine. Ten. Eleven. Twelve. Thirteen. Fourteen. Fifteen.

Will we ever see each other again? What if this is our last time? I take a deep breath and remind myself that this kind of thinking will get me nowhere.

"Aldi. Ari. It's time to leave," Mama reminds us that the line in front of us is leaving and she grabs our hands and holds them like someone holds their greatest possession.

She pulls out her empty wallet. And she takes out our IDs to hand them to the soldiers guarding the gate. Just like when we got here, they look through our belongings. They open our backpacks. They look through them. Then, they do a quick body scan–this time just like they do in the movies. We're out. We're walking. But a part of me is still behind that gate. And I don't know if that part will ever catch up.

A group of us—about a hundred are the lucky ones. We get to be free. Most people would be jumping and dancing. Not us. As we're exiting the gates of Hangari Concentration Camp, we are silent. All of us. Our feet lift up and down at the same time like they do in military films. We walk in rhythm. Not too fast. Not too slow. We just left, but my backpack is bringing down my shoulders. Arijana's only job is to carry her own weight. So far, she's doing great. We walk down the main street. We pass the Dom

Kulture, Opštinu, kiosk and little shops. Next, we pass my yellow brick school. My breathing becomes heavy and I sigh. Then I keep going. Arijana is quiet. She's playing with a tree branch that she picked from the ground.

We pass the houses and buildings. Some are burned down. Other homes are missing roofs. Windows. Doors. There's so much trash on the road. Most of the buildings are marked with shells. They're missing bricks with holes in them.

Some homes are spray painted with graffiti like Balije, Turci, Muslimani, derogatory terms for my people. Mama says be careful with your feet.

"Try not to step in blood stains. Da ne bi naograisali, nedo Dragi Allah," another phrase I hate hearing—God-forbid stepping into something will offend Allah and curse you.

The blood stains on the roads are silent reminders of genocide. They are reminders that someone, not long ago, walked, ran or danced on these streets. The only dancing that's happening now are souls holding hands and dancing kolo, a traditional Bosnian dance where people hold hands and dance in a circle. And the dancing of the crazed and drunk Croat militants.

Besides us, the lucky ones, and the soldiers navigating with rifles—every now and then—you can see a woman's or a child's face peeking through the curtains or standing on their verandas. In their eyes, there's greed. Hate. Maybe even regret? But it's too late for that. These women and children are living among the bad guys. They're eating with them. Sleeping with them. Laughing with them. Just like we did with our loved ones that are killed or locked in concentration camps.

16

Ice Cream and Ravens

Žepče, Bosnia and Herzegovina – Early July 1993

We've passed Čaršija and are now walking towards Preko. People are beginning to whisper. Then chat. Then sing. Some are smiling—we're safe! We're free! Some are crying—a different type of cry—unlike in that place. This is a happy cry. I don't know who started it, but we're all saying "Alhamdulillah," thanking God for setting us free.

I can't wait to get to Vranduk and see my other relatives. I can't wait to eat my aunt Tetka Besima's burek, her sirnica, her sarma. Tetak Asim makes the best cake rolls.

I can't wait to run around freely and play with my cousins. Arnela and Arnel. Haris and Adem. Jasmin.

Ever since the war began, our phone lines have been cut off. The post office has been closed. No word on the whereabouts of our uncles. Tetak Ibrahim. Tetak Brajko. Tetak Hamza. I don't know what's worse. Not knowing where your loved ones are—or leaving them behind in concentration camps or front lines.

Mama continues to hold onto us. Like when we were little. We pass the Catholic church. Next, Slastičarna, where we used to get ice cream from. I close my eyes. I stick my tongue out and I begin to lick.

"Aldi, what are you doing?" Mama looks at me confused.

"I'm licking my ice cream. It's so refreshing," I answer as I rub my hand and dry my wet mouth.

"Ice cream! What about me?" Arijana whines, as always.

"You, silly girls. Just wait. You'll get ice cream once we get to Vranduk." Mama interjects, her face convincing.

We continue to walk. We exit Čaršija, downtown. The beautiful mosque with munara—that used to echo muezzin's call for prayer.

We're crossing the bridge. I refuse to think about how Žepče, once a beautiful city—now a ghost town. I look down the bridge. I want to know what happened to the dead man from a couple days ago. His decomposing body is nowhere to be seen. How come? Every time I close my eyes. I see his remains. I saw him yesterday. Morning. Afternoon. Night. I saw him this morning. I see him now. Not in the river. In my head.

Scavengers—black ravens munching on what's left from the decomposing face, neck, back, arms, abdomen, legs and feet. His eyes maggot infested, and his nose cartilage exposed. His skin separating from the tissue and his boney knee popping through the ripped pants. That awful gassy odor. Me being stuck. There in that moment. Forever.

"Ice cream! Ice cream! I want ice cream!" Ari's voice draws me back to the now as she sings and hops toward the middle of the bridge, looking innocent.

17

When a Father Cries

Žepče, Bosnia and Herzegovina – Early July 1993

Arijana continues to sing the ice cream song. Each time a new tune—and a new dance. Mama looks relaxed. Not bothered by Ari's unmeasured excitement. And she lets her. We're approaching the finish line.

Just when we're all beginning to sing a victory song— BOOM! We all scream.

"Bastards! How could they? How could we trust them? Again. How naive of us to believe that they'd let us leave, just like that? Mater im," a male voice curses their mothers.

Mama shields our heads with her wide arms, like mothers do with their babies. Then another—BOOM! The sky tears open. Dust, fire, and screams fill the air. They're bombing us. Right here. On the bridge. My ears vibrate like someone is shouting inside my skull. I cover them with my pale, soaking palms. Makes no difference. First my ears. Then my whole body. Trembles like when Mama washes my pink teddy bear in a washing machine. Oh, how I miss him. How I wish he was here to comfort me.

Some of us fall flat on our bottoms, trying to duck or hide—but there's nowhere to go. Just open space and the river below. Someone crawls under a cart. Another grabs their chest and drops without a sound. I press my face into Mama's ribs and taste dirt in my mouth. I can't feel my feet. My whole body shakes like it's going to break apart.

It's louder than anything I've ever heard. Louder than thunder, louder than screams. My ears ring and the air burns my throat.

This must be it—the end.

"Girls, are you okay?" Mama asks, suffocating us with her kisses.

"Can we please leave now?" I ask her as I jiggle my foot.

"Yes," is all I get out of her.

Mama picks up Arijana. This time, I'm not jealous. I understand. I grab Ari's backpack and I hang it around my shoulder—like a big belly. Then, I run with two backpacks on me. No looking back. It's now. Or never.

I'm out of breath. My heart is loud and my forehead is wet. I wipe it with my sleeve. I see a woman run and then—she's gone. A flash, a sound, and she's chopped up like meat in a deli. Someone else is thrown into the air. I can hear. But I don't look. My brain won't erase what my eyes just witnessed. We run. And run. And run.

Alhamdulillah. By God's will and mercy, we make it across the bridge. To Preko.

My uncle Tetak Ibrahim waits for us. How did he know? In war, news travels quickly. No phones. No wires. No mailman. He opens his arms wide and lifts me up first. Then he lifts Arijana. Just the way it should always be. Me, first. Ari, next. Then–he lights up a cigarette and hands it to Mama. We're behind somebody's house. Not in the open.

He takes us inside some shed to get food and rest before we continue our journey to freedom.

"Anyone hungry for bread?" he asks with a smile that goes across his pleasant, tired face. Then, he breaks an entire loaf of bread in three equal pieces. One for each one of us. More bread than we've had in nine days—in there. It's like we died back on the bridge. And woke up in Bread Heaven.

I chew on the bread a few times. Just enough to push it down my throat. Then I do it again. And again. Afraid that if I take my time—someone will steal it from me. Like they stole my father. My innocence. My home. My childhood.

Ari finds a rubber duck on the ground. She bites her portion of the homemade wheat bread, with grains from Preko. Then she gives one to the ducky. Tetak and Mama catch up and I get up to stretch my legs. No longer in a state of panic. There are no Croats or Serbs here. No civilians—besides us.

Only our Bosniak soldiers. Only some holding rifles. Most unarmed. Smiling. Everything—our captors and torturers are not.

Mama and Tetak keep talking. I watch Arijana play with her rubber ducky, feeding crumbs of bread to tiny ants. I pretend I'm not listening to the grown ups' conversation. I listen with my ears. Not my eyes. I pick on my fresh scabs. And I watch my skin bleed—again. Not feeling pain. Somehow feeling lucky.

"It's true. My Keno. Only nineteen years old. Was shot. In his arm. Not one, not two, but ten shells in his bottom. June 30th—the day Žepče fell. The day they locked you up in that hell." Tetak pauses. He looks down. Then, up—like he's waiting for his answers to be found in the clouds.

There's something very strange in Tetak Ibrahim's eyes, his body language and voice. I don't know what it is. It puzzles me. There are no tears in his matte grey eyes. He's crying the saddest, invisible, silent cry. The kind that comes from the deepest place in person—the soul.

Mama pats him on his back. Takes a step forward like she wants to hug him. But she doesn't. Her fingers fidget like they don't know what to do. Or maybe—it's her. Maybe, she doesn't know what to do to ease Tetak's grief. I want to run up to him and give him the biggest hug there is. But I don't. I don't want them to know that I'm listening. That I'm snooping.

He's my Tetak. My aunt Azra's husband. And the only hugs that would take away the pain from his soul are the ones that can't reach him now—his sons. Keno. Adem. Haris. My cousins. All out of reach.

18

The Worst Sister in the World

Žepče, Bosnia and Herzegovina – Early July 1993

I'm pissed off.

My irresponsible, stupid sister did it again. I swear to God, this girl can't be trusted with a simple task! I want to choke her with my own two hands!

Her only job was to carry the little bag with our photo albums—our lives before the war. Photographs of Tata. Of us. Of our happy days. All gone, because of her.

"It's all her fault!" I scream, pointing at Ari with my index finger, kicking the air like I'm fighting invisible demons.

Tetak Ibrahim lifts me into his lap and wraps his arms around me. Mama does the same with Ari, who's crying—those honey eyes and long lashes drowning in tears. She's going to hate me forever. And honestly? I kind of hate myself too. Who in their right mind wants to strangle their own little sister?

Another secret to add to the list: I'm not just afraid I'm a bad sister—I'm convinced I might be the worst. Like, gold medal in the Sibling Shame

Olympics kind of the worst. I'd win and then immediately cry on the podium.

"Aldi, don't be so hard on yourself. You're still a child," Tetak whispers in my ear. "We all know you didn't mean it."

I wish that were true.

After Tetak helps me calm down, we set off toward Kiseljak and Previla. Mama doesn't yell at me. She doesn't even slap me. She does something worse—she ignores me. And so does Arijana.

I deserve it.

Tetak leads the way, his heavy rucksack packed with cans of food to deliver. Water canisters are tied around his neck and shoulders with rope. He looks like a walking donation center, and yet, he still puts one foot in front of the other. So do we.

We weave through destroyed houses and shattered fields. Criss-crossing, careful where we step. The snipers don't care if we're children. Little girls. Mothers. Grandparents. Disabled or sick. They don't see us as human.

Just Muslim. And apparently, that's enough to be hated. Enough to be hunted.

To avoid being seen, we stay out of the open. But that comes at a cost.

We're forced to take the paths of the dead—where the shells fell hardest, and the living rarely pass. We step over broken dog collars, fur soaked in blood. Kitties curled up like they're just napping. Cows with ribs showing. Horses with open eyes that no longer see.

Their only crime? Belonging to Bosniaks. To us.

19

Run, Aldi, Run

Žepče, Bosnia and Herzegovina – Early July 1993

Tetak Ibrahim packs more bread for the road. Three cans of food. And even two whole squares of keks—tea biscuits. One for me. One for Ari. For when we have a sweet tooth. I think keks sounds like "seks," a secret adult word. I don't know what it means, but it makes me giggle when I say it in my head.

We haven't had anything sweet in weeks—maybe longer? It gives me strength to keep going. I imagine walking on biscuits, cookies, cakes, and chocolate—my favorite food.

Ari isn't mad at me anymore. This is why I love her. She never stays mad, too long. Mama's still a little distant from earlier. But deep down, I think she gets it. I'm still a child too—just like Ari. Only three years older.

To show Mama I'm a good girl, I volunteer to carry the tote bag with all the goodies Tetak Ibrahim packed. I carry two backpacks—mine and Ari's. Ari carries the canister of boiled water. Mama takes the big travel rucksack that makes her back bend like she has a hump, plus another small tote bag with the rest of our things.

Our whole lives are packed on the backs of two of us—Mama and me. Tetak carries Arijana until Kiseljak. Then we part ways. Everything feels both frightening and strange. I don't fully understand the fighting or why we have to keep moving, but I know we have to stay together—Mama, Tetak, and me. Tetak is strong and quiet, carrying Arijana until Kiseljak before saying goodbye. I wonder why he has to stay when the world already feels so scary.

Mama tells me he is helping others, people just like us who have been trapped in terrible places, guiding them to safety even though the soldiers still shoot nearby. I don't know what "concentration camp" really means, but I know it isn't a place where anyone should stay.

The roads are blocked, and we have to climb up and down hills, walking where cars cannot go. My legs get tired, and sometimes I want to cry, but Mama holds my hand tight and says, "We're almost safe now." I look back once when Tetak stays behind, his face serious but calm. I feel proud and scared all at once.

We are just children caught in a war we don't understand, but somehow we keep moving forward because there are people like my uncle who won't leave anyone behind.

Previla is not just a hill—it feels like a mountain. My legs burn. My back hurts. The bag is too heavy, but I don't complain. Mama's holding Arijana's hand. I walk behind them. We don't talk. We just walk. Fast. Quiet. Careful.

Then—bang. A shot. Then another. We drop low.

"Run!" someone yells.

And we run. Like the ground's on fire. I hear more shots. They're trying to hit us. My heart is louder than the gunfire. My shoes slip on the dirt and rocks, but I keep going. I'm not stopping. I can't.

We hide behind a big rock. Mama's breathing hard. Arijana's crying. I hold her hand now. My knees are shaking.

Then we see someone—a young man coming up the hill with another guy.

Their faces are gray like the sky.

I recognize a neighbor. The other man looks familiar, but I don't know his name.

"Senada," he says to Mama. "I'm so sorry.

"Sorry for what?" Mama asks.

"It's Hamza. He didn't make it. They shot him... yesterday."

Mama covers her mouth. No scream. Just shuts her eyes.

"Šta će moja Majda? Kako će ona sama sa Anelom?"

Ari tugs at Mama's arm.

"What happened, Mama? Is Tetka Majda okay? What about Anela?"

"Nothing, baby," Mama whispers. "Keep walking."

The neighbor gives Mama a hug. "Majda and Anela will be okay. And so are you.

20

Crossing the Mountain

Žepče, Bosnia and Herzegovina – Early July 1993

I look up at Mama.

Her eyes are wet. But she doesn't cry. She just shakes her head from left to right. Then she mumbles, "Tzzz. Tzzzz. Tzzz." It sounds like her tongue is making music—beating the roof of her mouth like a drum. Like when someone is in denial. In shock. It makes my ears flinch and my heart feel small. Tetak Hamza was married to Mama's sister. He was an engineer. This man had brains bigger than America. And now—he's dead. Shot by a sniper in his head.

Tetak Hamza wasn't just an uncle—he was the smartest man in our family. His blue eyes, blond hair, and a smile that made everyone around him feel like they mattered. I remember how he'd bring gifts and teach me to blow the biggest bazooka bubbles, and I'd giggle, thinking he was invincible. He spoke English. German. French. And our mother tongue—Bosnian. That's four! But now, thinking of him, all I feel is a cold emptiness. He's gone. And so are the days when I could laugh without fear.

We lean back, digging our heels into the dirt, trying to slow ourselves down, but the rocks slip beneath our feet like ice. My heart races, and the earth beneath us seems to groan as if it's going to swallow us whole. We have to move fast. Every second feels like it could be our last

I still remember him dating Tetka Majda. He would pick her up from our house. Bring gifts. He taught me to blow the biggest bazooka bubbles in exchange for me letting Tetka Majda go out with him.

One night, long before the war, Mama, Tata, Tetak, Tetka and I went to Čaršija. There was music. Dancing. Singing. Food. And unlimited ice cream. He and Tetka were kissing. Holding hands. I wondered if Mama and Tata ever kissed like that. If they held hands.

I take another sip of water, chugging it down like this will be my last time. The sky is quiet for now. We sit down and take a break. Arijana eats, then drinks water. Mama and I only drink. There are so many tall trees. I only recognize pine and oak. We're at the top of this mountainous hill. Žepče looks so small from here. I try to find our house. All buildings and homes look like tiny insects. If only I had binoculars, maybe I'd see Daddy.

Now comes the hard part. We go down the hill. It's very steep and slippery. Rocks and dust slide under my feet. I lean back and dig my heels in, so I don't fall. Mama does too. My heart beats fast, and I feel scared.

A soldier carries Arijana on his back. He knows Tetak. He is from Preko, where it is still safe. He was never caught because he swam across the river to escape. He and other brave men keep Preko safe.

We slide down like stones in a stream. I feel scared, but I try to be brave because they are helping us.

Someone behind us screams. We turn just in time to see an older woman in our group lose her balance. She tumbles down, rolling like a log. Her body hits the ground hard. Her loved one cries out and runs after her.

She groans, clutching her leg. I think it's broken. But we can't stop for long. Not here. The shooting has stopped, but we know it's not over. Not really. Not yet.

We keep going, slipping and sliding. One slow step at a time. Down the mountain. Toward whatever's next.

21

Teacher Dana's Stick

Želeča-Begov Han, Bosnia and Herzegovina – Early July 1993

W e've made it to Želeča. Just before dark. Beat. Hungry. Thirsty. Alive. All three of us. We're finally safe. No more water left in our canister. A little creek waiting to feed our thirsty mouths. We drink with our hands shaped into cups. The water is clear. Cold as ice—so cold it stings my teeth—but I don't care.

We splash our faces. Our necks. Our arms and legs. Mama lets us wash our hair. It's the closest thing to a shower in forever. The dirt runs off in brown swirls. We watch it disappear down the stream like it was never there.

Then we keep walking toward Begov Han. The moon and stars are the only things lighting the way. No streetlights. No flashlights. Only our sparkly friends in the sky. I pretend the stars are following us. Protecting us.

We sleep in a school that smells like wet socks and dust. On cardboard boxes and one of those army-style-horse-colored blankets—the ones that itch. All the families packed into classrooms like sardines. Mama opens one small can of food. We each get a few spoonfuls. Tetak Ibrahim's bread is gone.

Another Bosniak soldier gives every family a dry food package. It looks weird. Tastes even weirder. Crackers. Hard ones. Sardines.

We're like sardines—stuffed in a tin, lying on a cold floor. I try not to cry. We're alive. That has to be enough for tonight.

A boy, a little younger than me, gets up. He looks around like he's not sure where to go. It reminds me of my first day of first grade, with teacher Dana—my father's first grade teacher too. A Bosnian Serb. I can still see it like it's happening right now. A boy in my class got up and walked toward the door.

"Where do you think you're going, young man?" Teacher Dana's voice cracked like thunder. Her face was puffy and deep red, like she was about to explode.

The boy said, "I have to pee!"

"If you want to go to the restroom," she snapped, "you must raise your hand and ask. You must stay in your seats until I give you permission to leave. Each time another adult walks in, you must stand up and wait until you're told to sit. Do we all understand? Those who can't follow rules will stand in the corner with their backs to the class. No talking. No moving. And if you still can't behave—get ready for this stick. Your palms will hear it. Never forget it. Or an ear pull. Or a hair pull. That will teach you a lesson. Any questions?"

Then she barked at the boy, "Now go back to your seat. Let's practice."

Everyone burst out laughing. I remember laughing too. Teacher Dana went right back to lecturing us about rules. It makes me laugh now—even here. Even in this school with itchy blankets and hungry bellies.

The cardboard under my back crinkles every time I move. The blanket scratches my skin. Arijana keeps coughing in her sleep. I wrap my arm around her. She's shivering.

I whisper, "Pretend we're camping."

She doesn't answer. But she scoots closer. That's enough. I look around the room. There's a woman rocking a baby who won't stop crying. A man sitting in the corner staring at nothing. Someone is praying quietly, whispering words I can't understand. I try not to cry. We're alive.

22

Muezzin's Voice

Begov Han, Topčić Polje, Nemila, Vranduk, Bosnia and Herzegovina – Early July 1993

Another packaged expired meal. We eat. At least we try. This one is worse than last night's. I don't even know what I'm eating. I'm disgusted by it. But I eat. And eat. And eat. Stuffing my face, like I'm trying to shove down the hurt.   Like maybe if I'm full enough, it'll push the sadness away. Like maybe I'll get food poisoning, and it'll all just end. Here. Now.

The expired meal gets to me. It comes out of my nostrils. My mouth. Chopped up. Blood red like my Bosna i Hercegovina. Someone passed down baking soda. And a metal cup of water. I drink. It's supposed to help.

We grab our belongings. Hang them up around us. Fill up the canister water. A large group of us begins to walk towards Zenica. Refugees. Our whole lives, packed in these bags and backpacks. The roads are safe. No Serbs and Croats. No cars. Only a military vehicle every now and then. Checkpoints. Us—walking the walk to freedom.

We pass Topčić Polje. Here we rest. Our neighbors from Berek are staying with their relatives. The wife makes lemonade for us kids. Then, she boils water and pours it over finely ground coffee beans. She serves the coffee in a hand carved copper coffee pot, straight from Baščaršija. Turkish coffee. Bosnian way. With rahat lokum, a sugary rectangular confection. And she serves kocka, sugar cubes in a copper serving dish, matching the pot. Just smaller. Mama takes a bite of rahat lokum.

Ari eats kocka, as if it was a bar of chocolate. She almost chokes on it. Mama gives her water to wash it down. I save mine. For you never know. I take my right hand and I gently pat it on Ari's back. Something that I've seen grown-ups do when someone is choking on food. Mama smokes not one—but five hand-rolled cigarettes. She seems like she's in the clouds. I don't get it. I hate cigarettes. They stink. They make me cough. And irritate my asthma. But who cares. Everyone around me smokes, as if smoking will make everything better.

We continue to walk towards Nemila, one town before our final destination—Vranduk—the old city. I can't feel my legs. Never, ever, have I walked this much. It's humid. The sun is bright and it's moving towards the west. Changing colors. Looking orangish. I sniff my armpits. Then I sniff Arijana's. We're about the same. Mama's don't need sniffing. You can smell them walking next to her. I don't know if the sweat or the cigarette smell is worse. Together, they make you puke.

Mama's getting nervous. It's late afternoon. We must get to Vranduk before night falls. Ari stalls. She lays on the hot ground and refuses to get up.

"Ari—get up. Mom's going to yell if you don't. Give me your hand. I'll pull you. We'll pretend to be a train," I try to encourage her to continue.

"Fine! We'll play this dumb game," she answers in an irritable voice.

"Choo. Choo. Choo. Chooo," I lead. She follows. Mama smiles.

We're in Nemila, such an ugly name for a nice-looking town. A dark-skinned man with brown hair, brown eyes, and a salt-and-pepper beard—taller than Father—recognizes us. One of our aunt and uncle's neighbors. He's in a horse cart, picking up food, hygiene things, and supplies for Vranduk. He offers us a ride. His horse leads. We climb up onto the wooden cart. We sit. We yeehaw away like cowboys in a horse carriage, leaving the war behind us—for now.

We ride through a pitch-black tunnel that smells like mold. Then another tunnel. Creepy. Our eyes are wide, but we don't see. Kind of like the Serbs and Croats. I wonder how the black and white horse can see. I bet his ears are his guide.

We arrive. It's Akšam time. A muezzin recites the adhan, calling all believers to pray their evening prayer. It's magical. Calming. Makes my heart want to jump out. Makes my legs want to face Allah. Stand up straight, right hand over my left, covering my chest. Bending down. Touching my knees. Straightening my spine.

And my favorite—touching the warm Egyptian rug with my bare hands. Pressing my face into it, soft and full of prayers, whispering, "Subhan Rabbiy al-A'la." Glory be to my Lord, Most High.

23

From Tunnels to Towers

Vranduk, Bosnia and Herzegovina – Early July 1993

Vranduk. The views here—are the kind from a fairytale Mama used to tell, about real kings and queens, sultans and sultanas. We exit the tunnel and climb up the steep, mountainous macadam road. By the time we reach the top, the adhan from the minaret fades into the wind.

Crushed stone on our path makes our bottoms bounce like we're on a carnival ride. Ari and I laugh. This is the most fun we've had in months.

To our left and right, green mountains hug the village. Trees packed tight like soldiers on guard, protecting us—in all shades of green, my favorite color. We pass the old cemetery. I quietly recite El-Fatiha for the souls resting there. Ari plays with a daisy she picked up in Nemila. Mama chats with the neighbor.

Below, the Bosna River flows—calm and glittering—like it's trying to keep Vranduk safe. A railroad runs nearby, quiet as in my Teacher Dana's classroom. It feels strange not to hear a train's choo-choo, or see waving hands through glass windows.

At the very top, an ancient fortress sits tall, proud of its rich history. Watching over us like it has for a thousand years. Illyrian and Celtic roots. Roman rule. Slavic migration. The rise of the Kingdom of Bosnia. Ottoman conquest. Austro-Hungarian takeover. World War II. The Yugoslav era. And now—this war. The Bosnian War.

I enjoy the bumpy ride toward Tetka's house. The air is cool and smells sweet—like wet earth and wildflowers. After everything we've seen, Vranduk feels peaceful. Like home before the war. A home we no longer have.

Our old neighbors—the Croats—live in it now. Sleeping in our beds. Using our furniture. Driving our cars. Eating our food. Wearing our jewelry. Spending our money.

Red roofs cover the houses, just like in Žepče. Some homes are new. Others are as ancient as my Nana Điha. How I miss her. I hope she's okay. I hope she gets exchanged. I hope she escapes the concentration camp like we did.

We make it to the top. The neighbor stops the carriage and lets us off.

Our aunt and uncle's gray brick house is just around the corner, on the other side of the fortress. Their red roof faces it—like it's keeping watch.

In the yard, my cousins—Arnela, Arnel, Jasmin, Adem, and Haris—are playing soccer. My cousin Keno—alive. Wounded. But alive. If only Tetak Ibrahim knew. My aunts—Tetka Besima, Tetka Fatima, and Tetka Azra—and my uncle Tetak Asim are waiting, arms open.

The boys spot us first. Arnel grabs the ball. They push each other, racing to reach us.

I drop our bags on the cobblestone ground and run. My feet feel light. No longer tired.

Everyone hugs at once—even the boys, who usually only high five. My aunts run to us too. I'm suddenly wrapped in arms and kisses—my cheeks smothered in pink and red lipstick. It's more love than I've had in months.

It makes me feel wanted. Loved—but guilty. Why? Don't know. Lots of tears. Happy. And sad.

24

Who Needs a Shower Anyway?

Vranduk, Bosnia and Herzegovina – Early July 1993

It's awfully peaceful here. No explosions. No screaming. No smell of smoke. It makes me feel...afraid. Afraid that the bombing and shooting will sneak up behind my back when I least expect it.

Back in Žepče, I could smell danger. See it. Hear it. Here—I can't. And that scares me. What if they attack us without any warning? What then?

Tetka's house is small. Three rooms. An unfinished bathroom and basement. The toilet works, but there's no bathtub. No shower. Just pipes and tiles and hope. No ice cream. No burek. Little food.

Soon after we got here, the rest of the family, those we left behind barbed wire—arrived too. They let them go.

My seventy-year-old Nana couldn't walk, so they pushed her in a wheel-barrow. And uncle Tetak Esad came with them.

Lucky for them—they got to walk on the main roads. Not across Previla. Not under bullets. Not like us. Makes me feel strong. Fearless. Like a hero from American movies.

Tetka's home was built for four. Now twenty-two of us live inside. Sometimes it feels like Begov Han again. Or the camp. No beds. Just a blanket on the floor, and another one on top. Four of us under the same cover.

The boys sleep in one room. The girls in another. Moms get the third room. Tetak Asim and my 18-year-old Cousin Keno—two grown men—sleep outside on the balcony.

At night, I count breathing. Snoring. Whispers. Farts. So many people. So little space. But still—no bombs. Just peace that feels like it might shatter any second.

Most people here are farmers. They grow their own food. Food that they must not waste and save for a Nedaj Bože—God forbid—moment. My aunt and uncle are not farmers. They don't have land. No crops to pick. No cows to milk. No chickens to collect eggs. Nothing to eat. Most days, we only have one meal. Corn or wheat homemade bread from the flour that the neighbors gift. Bean, cabbage, lentil soup. No burek, sirnica, ice cream or aunt Tetak Asim's cake rolls.

Some days are better than others. If we're lucky, we get two meals a day. We eat very little. And after two weeks, our clothes become loose. Before the war, Mama had about ninety kilos. None of her clothes fit anymore. They hang loose. Her high cheeks are deflated like a balloon. Flat. On the days we get two meals, Mama gives her second meal to me and Ari. It doesn't help. Our bellies still make noise.

Our moms divide the chores. Some cook. Others wash the dishes. Some vacuum, mop, or dust. A few stand outside by the big metal tubs, hand washing laundry in freezing water. Then others hang the wet clothes on lines that stretch between trees. Some fold.

Ari plays outside with our cousins and the neighbor kids. Sometimes, I join them—but only after I help Mama wash everyone's clothes in the ice-cold water.

She hates it when my hands turn purple from scrubbing. But I tell her I don't mind. I say I'd rather keep her company than play. That's not the whole truth.

But I say it anyway. I want to run around and play too. But I feel bad for Mama. She does the most work. There are twenty-two of us—that's at least twenty-two outfits a day! Good thing we only change clothes twice a week. Sometimes once. Not enough soap to change every day. Not enough outfits either.

Since we don't have a real shower and it's summer, we bathe in the outside toilet downstairs. Once a week. We take turns.

Taking a shower is like a mission. First, we boil a big pot of water. Then we carry it—carefully—down the stairs. After that, we bring down a plastic baby tub. We mix the boiling water with cold water from the concrete sink outside. Once it's the right temperature, we carry the tub into the outhouse.

We use a plastic cup to pour the water. No shampoo. No conditioner. Just the same bar of soap we use for laundry. There's a hole in the ground where we go to the bathroom. No way to flush the poop or the pee. So we squeeze our noses. Every time we shower. Or go. But at least we're free. And alive.

25

Like Mama's Medicine

Vranduk, Bosnia and Herzegovina – August 1993

Mama takes care of Hasinica, my aunt's cranky, ancient grandmother with facial hair and a long gray mustache—in exchange for food and hygiene products. Hasinica almost never comes out of her room. And when she does, she yells at us kids. All of us—except Arnela. Never Arnela.

She gives Arnela lollipops, kocka, and fruit as if sugar coating will make her more lovable.

Arnela is just a little younger than me, but ever since we all moved into her home, she's been hiding things from us—her toys, her pretty dresses, her sparkly hair clips, hair ties, brushes, combs, nail polishes, eyeshadows, and lipsticks. All the things I used to have. I miss my home. I miss my toys. I miss my pink Teddy. I miss my Daddy.

Hasinica isn't a Serb or a Croat, but I'm still afraid of her. I'm glad she's not my grandmother. Who cares about lollipops, fruit and kocka!

Each week, Tetak Asim, Keno, Edo, and Adem leave. I don't know where they go, but they always look serious. They take the donkey with them. A few days later, they come back—quiet, tired. The donkey carries things we need to survive: oil, flour, sugar, coffee, cigarettes. Food. Supplies. Hope in bags.

They must go to the pijaca—the market—or trade with villagers in nearby towns. We never ask. We just wait for the donkey to return. Sometimes, they talk about sweet things they saw—baklava, hurmašice, krempite, cakes that look like the ones from our birthdays. But we never get to try them. Whatever money or profit they make, we use it only for necessities. Never for desserts. Never for fun. Just enough to keep us alive until the next trip.

I spend most of my free time helping Mama or hanging out in the fortress. Taking walks. Writing in a brown, lined notebook Tetka Besima gave me. She said it was for school, but I don't use it for math or grammar. I use it to empty my head. Because if I don't clear my head, I'll never use Mathematics or Grammar.

We're safe and alive, but I don't feel it. Not really. I try to stay busy. Nobody asks me to. I just do it. I pick up dirty laundry. Hang and fold clothes. Organize shoes. Sweep. Mop. Anything to keep my hands moving.

Doing things slows down my brain. It numbs the ache inside—like an anesthetic. Like Mama's pills, but for my thoughts.

Other kids don't care about neatness or being clean. As long as their bellies are full, they laugh, play, and run. I wish I could be like them. Just care about myself. But I can't. I'm not like them.

At night, I stay up listening to Mama and the aunts whisper and cry. I watch their hands, their eyes, their tired bodies. I read their sadness like I used to read bedtime stories. And it breaks me.

So, I take it on myself—to help. To make things just a little easier. I can't give them back our house. Or Daddy. Or peace. But maybe I can give them a swept floor. A folded sheet. A moment less heavy. I write about it in my notebook. It's the only place I tell the truth. Sometimes I write letters to God. Sometimes to Daddy. But mostly to myself.

Dear Notebook,

Today I folded all the laundry before anyone asked me. I even found all the missing socks. I lined up the shoes by the door, swept the crumbs, and wiped the table three times. Mama didn't notice. But maybe she felt it. Maybe her feet were a little less tired because of me. I saw her cry again last night. She tried to hide it, but I saw her shoulders shaking under the blanket. I didn't say anything. I just listened. I miss our house.

I envy Arnela. It's not enough that she's prettier than me–she also has everything I don't. Sometimes. I'm jealous of the dead for being spared continuous suffering, grief and fear.

I Miss My Pink Teddy.

"Can I play with your bear?" I ask Arnela, trying my best puppy eyes.

She pretends not to hear me. Runs straight to her father like I'm invisible.

I swear, I could punch her. I could yank her ponytail, throw her down, make her cry until her nose bleeds.

But I don't.

Instead, I wait for night.

When the others are asleep, when the snores start and the whispers die down, I tiptoe across the room and grab her ugly bear. I squeeze it hard—not like I used to squeeze mine, soft and close, like a friend. This one, I squeeze with hate. Rage. Revenge.

Then I spot her Barbie. The blonde one. With shiny hair and eyes just like hers. I snatch it quietly and hide under my blanket. I change its outfit.

Pull off her skirt. Swap shoes. I pretend Barbie is Arnela and I'm the boss now. But when I try to bend her arm, it snaps off.

Panic.

My heart races. I try to snap it back on, but the plastic joint is cracked. It won't fit. The arm is ruined.

"Who's up?" Tetak Asim's voice slices the dark.

I freeze. My body stiffens. I tiptoe back to my corner and curl up, pretending to sleep.

In the morning, Arnela wakes up screaming.

"My Barbie! Who broke my Barbie?!"

She cries like the world ended, hugging the one-armed doll and sobbing to her dad.

I don't say anything at first. But Tetak Asim keeps glancing at me. I can tell he knows. He saw me last night. I can feel it in his eyes—the kind of look that burns.

So, I say it. "It was me," I whisper. "I broke it. It was an accident."

His eyes narrow. His mouth stays tight. He's never hit me before, but I think maybe this time he will.

And if he does, Mama won't stop him. She'll say, "Neka je, sama si kriva." You brought it on yourself. She always says that.

"Udaraj mojom rukom," she once told someone. Hit her with my hand.

That's how it works. Adults can hurt you if you mess up. Especially if you admit it.

I miss Tata's voice. I miss bananas. Real ones. Yellow gold. I dream about peeling one and biting it in three bites flat.

I miss just being a kid.

But if I keep helping and acting like a good girl, maybe Mama will cry less. Maybe, my secrets will be safe.

If I keep writing, maybe I won't forget who I was before the war.

If I keep dreaming, maybe one day my dreams might come true.

And if I just keep moving—keep going—maybe I won't break.

26

Ten Reasons Not to Jump

Vranduk, Bosnia and Herzegovina – September 1993

S ome days, there's nothing to eat. At least we still have water. On days like that, we steal fruit from the neighbors—cherries, apples, raspberries, strawberries. We never get caught. It's almost like they don't care. Like they understand. Like they know hunger well enough not to punish it.

Because food and supplies are so scarce, and we're always hungry, Nana Điha, Tetka Azra, and Tetka Fatima decide to leave. So do their kids. They found an abandoned Serb home in Begov Han. That's seven fewer mouths to feed. A little more food for us. A little more space to sleep. A little less noise in the house, but a lot more silence in my head.

It's September now. School starts. Mama enrolls us in the local school across the river. We walk there. We have no supplies—just my brown notebook and my old backpack from Žepče. The teachers are kind. The kids... not so much. They stare. They whisper. I feel like an outsider. Like an alien dropped from the sky.

Our clothes are donations. Hand-me-downs with holes. Too big. Too small. My shoes flap when I walk. My hair itches like crazy. Not just regular itchy from not washing—it's worse. I scratch all the time. Behind my ears. My neck. My scalp. I'm a walking itch.

My teacher notices. She asks me to stay after class.

Then she hands me a small plastic bottle.

"It'll help with the bugs. Just take it. Make sure your whole family uses it," she says, smiling.

"What bugs?" I ask, scratching again.

"Aldi... you have lice," she says gently. "This shampoo will help. And use this brush. It'll help get them out." She pats my back. My face burns.

I want to disappear. I want the floor to open up and swallow me whole. I hate being a refugee. I hate my clothes. I hate my shoes. I hate my dirty, lice-infested hair. I hate everything. And everyone. My life sucks.

"Thank you. I'll give it to my Mama," I say quickly, already walking toward the door.

"Wait—just a second," Teacher says, grabbing a plastic bag. "Here. Some school supplies. For you."

"Thank you," I mumble, not looking up. My eyes stay down. My feet rush out.

Instead of going home, I climb up to the fortress. The old stone walls overlook the river, the village, the trees turning gold. The sky is too blue for how I feel.

I climb onto the highest rock. I look down.

I think about jumping. About how quick it would be. About how everything might just stop. The hunger. The shame. The fear.

I stand there for a long time. My feet planted. My arms tight to my sides. My mind racing.

Ten Reasons Why I Should Jump:

    1. *I'm tired of scratching my scalp until it bleeds.*

    2. *I hate being dirty all the time.*

    3. *My clothes smell like someone else's past.*

    4. *The kids at school look at me like I'm trash.*

    5. *I miss my old life.*

    6. *I hate this new one.*

    7. *No one listens.*

    8. *No one sees me.*

    9. *Even lice won't leave me alone.*

    10. *I feel like nothing will ever get better.*

Ten Reasons Why I Shouldn't Jump:

  1. *Mama would cry.*

  2. *Arijana would think it was her fault.*

  3. *I haven't seen Tata since the escape.*

  4. *Who would help Mama?*

  5. *I want to write a book one day.*

  6. *I want to see snow again.*

  7. *I want to eat a banana without sharing.*

  8. *I want to wear clean clothes that fit.*

  9. *I want to kiss someone someday.*

  10. *I don't want to disappear. Not really.*

A soft breeze tugs at my sleeves. I step back from the edge. My legs are shaking. My heart is a drum in my chest. I sit on the stone wall, legs dangling. I decide. I won't jump. Not today. Maybe not ever. But I won't tell anyone what I almost did.

This secret is mine. Like the bugs in my hair. Like the broken dreams in my chest. Like the FBI in me.

Everything has an expiration date. Human life. Food. Hunger. Lice. Illness. Happiness. Love. Tragedy. This too shall pass. Expire. And no matter how bad things get they'll get better. They always do. At least temporary. Like this circular life. The shape of our planet. The shape of the universe. The shape of mothers' bellies that bring life. And the shape of the soil that buries.

27

Scabs and Snipers

Vranduk, Bosnia and Herzegovina – October 1993

Aunt Strina, Edo, Ado, and the three of us sleep downstairs in Hasinica's unfinished basement. No running water. No electricity. No plumbing. Just a wood-burning stove and two old ottoman sleepers—one for us, one for Strina.

The room smells like mold and feels like it's waiting for death. Like Hasinica upstairs, talking to herself. Arguing with invisible people. Farting without care. Making us laugh.

Not everyone at school cares how I look. Old rags don't bother them. They don't ask questions when I show up with no lunch. Some even offer to share theirs with me.

Of course, I can't take it. How could I? What kind of person would that make me? So, I always say, "Thanks, I already ate."

It's easier to lie than to tell the truth. Nobody needs to know we're starving.

I like going to school. It's the only normal thing I have left. There's a routine. A rhythm. A world where things make sense. A world where I make sense.

At school, I feel like I'm in control. I got this.

I may not have a home, or enough food, or nice clothes—or my father, but I got this.

So, I take notes. I memorize. I read and study, just to prove to them—and to myself—that I've got brains. That I matter. And I get good grades. The teachers like me. They respect me. And that? That makes me feel good.

We don't have textbooks. Each day, the teachers dictate the lessons, and we copy them into our notebooks.

We have a group project. Everyone votes on where to meet. I silently pray it's anywhere but Tetka's. It's too loud, too cramped, too embarrassing. But my prayer doesn't work.

When they choose our place, I panic. I try to get out of it. I lie and say my cousin is sick. But they don't care. They want to come. They want to see where I live.

And they do.

The night before, I don't sleep. I lie in the cold room, under a thin blanket, staring at the ceiling. The fire burned out hours ago, and the air bites. Still, I sweat. My tracksuit is damp. My hair clings to my forehead. Not from heat—but from shame. From fear. From the weight of tomorrow.

They arrive. Four of them. Smiling, curious. I open the door. Embarrassed. They step in. Eyes scan the clutter. The peeling walls. The smell of wood smoke and boiled cabbage. Nobody says anything. But I feel it. Their silence is loud.

We go to Tetka's bedroom and we sit on the floor with our notebooks. No table. No chairs. Just knees and a cold floor. Mama brings tea in mismatched cups. One is chipped.

They sip politely. I don't. My stomach's twisted. We finish quickly. They leave even faster.

No goodbye hugs. Just awkward smiles.

I don't walk them out. I just close the door and sink to the floor.

"They seem nice," Mama says.

"They are," I answer.

"Now, could you freaking leave me alone for only a minute," I ask Mama.

"Sure, Aldi." She exits and closes the door. I take a pillow and I scream my heart into it.

A week later, my body breaks out in scabies. The itch is worse than the lice. It spreads everywhere. We shower less now—it's too cold. And the less I shower, the more I itch. I scratch so much, the red marks turn purple. It spreads to Ari too.

The teachers tell us to stay home. Until it clears. Until we're not contagious. All of the kids and the adults get it. One by one.

Nobody wants to play with us. They keep their distance.

Then—my uncle Tetak Ibrahim is killed.

So is Tetak Brajko.

My aunts go from denial, to anger, to bargaining, to crying. Stuck somewhere between depression and screaming in their sleep.

They grieve with everything they have. Crying. Cursing. Wailing. Fainting.

When they first found out—they collapsed. Dropped

to the floor. Pale. Breathless. Like they had died too.

I keep seeing that moment. Them on the ground. Still. Tetak Ibrahim was shot. A sniper. He kneeled to pick up a can of food. One second there. The next—gone. A father. A husband. A son. A brother. An uncle. Vanished. Like a feather blown away by wind.

Tetka Fatima is stuck in denial. She refuses to believe Tetak Brajko is really gone. He isn't coming back.

There are three versions of his death.

First—they say he was badly wounded, taken to a hospital in Zagreb, Croatia. Maybe still alive?

Second—they say he was found dead, lying in a bathtub of an abandoned house in Preko.

Third—they say a local man found his body and

buried him in the cemetery.

No one knows which story is true. And maybe that's worse than knowing for sure.

Tetka Fatima clings to the first story. The one where he's still alive. Where someone took care of him. Saved him. She talks about Zagreb like it's right around the corner. Like he could walk through the door any minute.

She doesn't cry much. Not like Tetka Azra. She just stares out the window. Talks to herself. Folds and unfolds his t-shirt. Just in case.

Sometimes, I catch her whispering his name. Softly. Like a prayer. I don't know which story is true. But I know the truth hurts, no matter how you hear it.

I miss him too. His loud voice. His jokes. The way he called me "Aldi." The way he carried my cousin Jasmin on his back like he was a magic horse from fairy tales and Jasmin was the little boy on a mission to find treasure. He was strong. Always laughing.

Now it's too quiet. Tetka Fatima's silence is the loudest sound in the house.

28

Maybe I'm Possessed by Jinns?

Vranduk, Bosnia and Herzegovina – November 1993

My father's older brother, Amiđa Nurija, is free. They let him out.

We walk down the hill to the train tracks to wait for Amiđa to arrive. All of us. Strina, Edo, and Ado stand at the front. Waiting. Their bodies are uneasy. Fidgeting. So lucky.

The train pulls in. Stops. People start coming out. We wait, hearts pounding.

Then—there he is. Smiling. Waving. He rushes toward Strina and kisses her on the lips. She hugs him tight. They're both crying. Tears of happiness.

He looks nothing like himself. Too thin—like a skeleton. There are bandages on his forehead. His clothes hang off his body, held up by a rope tied around his waist so they don't fall. His hair is grey now.

This isn't the same Amiđa I saw just a few months ago. The one I remember had dark hair. Muscles. Strength. The man in front of me is older. Skinnier. Broken. He looks...defeated.

My chest feels tight. Like I'm swallowing rocks. I don't know if I should hug him or cry. Maybe both. He smiles at me, but his eyes don't match.

They look far away—like he's still inside the camp, even though he's physically standing with us.

Strina won't stop crying. She holds onto him like she's afraid he'll disappear again. Edo and Ado cling to his legs. And I just stand there. Frozen. Staring.

I want to ask him if it was scary. If they hurt him. If he ate. If he slept. But no words come out. I can't speak. I can't breathe. All I can do is stare at the man who used to be my uncle and wonder if pieces of him are still lost behind those barbed wire fences.

I'm sad. Sad to see him like this. Sad that this is what freedom looks like. A skeleton in baggy clothes held up by rope. Bandages on his head. Missing teeth. Bruises all over his skin and bones. Gray hair where it used to be black. Eyes that don't smile, even when his mouth tries to.

I'm sad because this means the camps are real. Worse than I imagined. And if this is what Amiđa Nurija looks like after getting out...what does that mean for my Tata? He's still there. Still locked up. Still waiting.

I want to ask about him. I want to shout, *Where is my dad?* But I don't. I just swallow the lump in my throat and stand there, watching everyone hug and cry.

I don't want this to be my life. I want my old life back. My home. My dad. My family without rope belts and bruises.

But mostly, I want to stop feeling this heavy sadness that never goes away.

We all walk to Tetka Besima's house. Up the hill. Ado pisses me off. He's holding Amiđa's hand like he's proud. Like he wants me to see. Like he's saying, *Look, my dad is back and yours isn't.* I am jealous. Of the living. Of the dead. It's not fair. His dad came back. Mine is still locked up.

Edo notices. He walks beside me without saying a word. I'm glad. I don't want to talk. I just keep walking, staring at the ground, imagining the train. Imagining my dad getting off. *Would he look like Amiđa? Gray hair? Skin and bones? Would he even be able to walk?*

Stop it, I tell myself. Don't go there.

When we get to Tetka's house, everyone goes inside. I don't. I can't. I grab my journal and disappear into the fortress. My secret place. My safe place.

I write my heart out. I scream onto the page. I shout with my pen. Then I climb the fortress wall. I stand there, high above everything. I hold the paper close and recite all the surahs I know: El-Fatiha. An-Nas. Al-Falaq. The words tremble in my mouth, but I say them anyway.

Then I make a promise to myself. If I ever get like this again—if the darkness comes back and climbs in with me—I'll talk to Imam.

Maybe I'm possessed by jinns. Maybe I messed up, možda sam nao-graisala, like Tetka Fatima once said when her eyes went glassy and her hands wouldn't stop shaking.

I don't jump. I climb down. Quietly. Carefully. And I keep the list hidden in my notebook, like a secret that saved me.

29

The Letter and the Hunger

Vranduk, Bosnia and Herzegovina – December 1993

It's cold. Outside and inside. The roads are icy and unclean. Everyone stays indoors. We fight over who gets to sit closest to the wood-burning stove. We fight for food. The moms are always cranky. They yell. We yell. It's like we're fighting our own war—against each other. Against the very people we love.

On days when the snow piles too high, school is canceled. We stay home. I'd rather walk barefoot through the snow—no boots, no snow pants, no warm jacket—than be locked inside. It reminds me too much of back there.

Amiđa brought a letter from Father. And a rolled cigarette—a gift for Mama. *I love you* was written on it.

Dear Senada, Aldi, and Ari,

I miss you. I'm okay. Don't worry about me. They treat me fine. I wrote before. I know you wrote too, but I didn't get any of your letters. Keep writing. Maybe one of these days, I'll get your letter. Hugs and kisses.

Love, Tata

Amiđa Nurija is sick. He coughs constantly—deep, raw coughs—spitting up blood. He can't eat. Has no energy. They say he has tuberculosis. So does Tata—but his isn't this bad.

That he has little chance of surviving. That's why they let him out. Freedom in exchange for a slow death.

I don't want him to die. I don't want to see another dead body. Not another uncle buried. Not in my dreams. Not when my eyes are wide open.

He's been throwing up for days. He doesn't eat. So, he gives his food to Ado and Edo. Ari and I just watch them chew. Watch them swallow. Like watching will somehow feed our own hungry bellies.

"I wish my dad was here to give me his food," Arijana says, tears running down her flat cheeks.

Mama turns her head. I know she's crying. Amiđa and Strina's faces shift. They pretend they didn't hear her.

"Ari, here's mine."

I give her the rest of my bread. Then, I grab my journal and write, *I hate Ado. Edo. Arnel. Arnela. Their fathers are here. And ours isn't.*

Then I cross it out. It's not their fault. None of this is. But I still feel it—this fire in my chest. Because I'm hungry. And angry. And tired of pretending I'm okay. Mama, Amiđa Nurija, Strina, Tetka Besima, and Tetak Asim are all sitting together in the small room by the stove. The air smells of burning wood and cold.

Strina sighs and says, "I miss keks, those sweet sugar biscuits we used to eat."

Mama laughs softly, shaking her head. "I miss sex."

Everyone stops for a moment. Then the grown-ups burst out laughing, loud, crazy laughter that fills the room. Even we kids start giggling, not really knowing why it's so funny but laughing anyway.

My older boy cousins laugh their asses off like lunatics, like they know exactly what sex is.

"What's sex?" I whisper to Arnela.

She shrugs. "I think it's a secret adult word."

"I want to know," I say, but then I giggle again. It sounds too much like keks.

The laughter doesn't last long, but for a few seconds the room feels lighter, like the war is far away.

30

She Gave Me What I Broke

Vranduk, Bosnia and Herzegovina – Mid-December 1993

It's winter break, and we're leaving for Zenica. They say Zenica is full of refugee shelters—people from Srebrenica, Živinice, Kozarac, Prijedor, Banja Luka, and other cities. They also say that two meals a day are guaranteed.

Mama's had enough. Enough of watching her children starve. If we stay, we'll all wither away. If we leave, at least there's a chance—some chance—of surviving the winter.

We pack what little we have. A change of clothes. The brown notebook. The lice shampoo. The letter from Tata. Mama wraps bread in a towel and tucks it deep in her bag. Ari and I don't ask questions. We know better by now.

The morning is dark and cold. Snowflakes fall quietly, like my tears when everyone is asleep. Tetka Besima hugs us tight and slips something into Mama's hand. A few coins. Maybe more. Mama doesn't look. Just nods.

We step outside in our hand-me-down tennis shoes, refugee donation spring coats, and ripped hats that barely cover our ears. The snow bites at our ankles.

Just as we start down the path, Arnela bursts out the door behind us, still in her pajamas.

"Čekaj!" she calls asking us to wait, running through the snow in socks. Her breath clouds in front of her.

She reaches us, cheeks red, holding out a white warm puffy jacket.

"Here—this is for you," she says, shoving it into my arms before I can say anything.

Then she turns to Ari and kneels down. "And these are for you," she says, sliding a pair of red winter boots onto the ground. "They're a little big, but they'll keep you warm."

Ari stares at the boots like they're magic.

"Thank you," I whisper, my throat tight.

Arnela nods, her big ocean blue shiny eyes filling with something between guilt and goodbye.

Then she adds, almost in a whisper, "You can keep the Barbie too. I know...it broke. But it's okay. You can have it."

I stare at her, stunned. The Barbie I broke. The one I stole in a fit of jealousy. Her kindness pierces me deeper than any slap could.

"I'm sorry," I say, barely able to speak.

"It's okay," she says, looking down. "I get it. You didn't ask to come here. And I didn't ask for my house to turn into a shelter."

We stand in silence for a moment.

"I forgive you," she adds. Then she runs back toward the house, leaving footprints in the snow and a piece of her heart with us.

I don't hate her. Never did. Never will. I only wanted what she had. And I didn't. But now I see we ruined her peace too. We came into her life like a storm, uninvited and impossible to ignore.

We walk to the main road where buses are supposed to stop. But nothing is on time in war. We wait. Our toes numb. Our breath, invisible in the air. Mama wraps her scarf around Ari's face, then mine.

Finally, a bus shows up. Rusted. Overcrowded. We squeeze in. I sit on Mama's lap. Ari leans into her side. The ride is long and bumpy. Nobody talks. Everyone stares ahead or closes their eyes. Some cry quietly. Some pray. I press my face against the foggy window and watch the whiteness blur by. Trees like bones. Villages like ghosts. We stop. Then go again. Stop. Go. At a checkpoint, soldiers get on. Their boots stomp up and down the aisle. One shines a flashlight in Mama's face. She doesn't flinch.

When we finally arrive in Zenica, it's almost noon. People are everywhere. The shelter is loud. Cold air seeps through the cracks in the windows. We get a bed and blankets—the gray and itchy ones. We put our bags under the bed. Then we head to the kitchen. To wait in line.

There's soup. Hot soup. With noodles. And bread. And just like that, Zenica becomes our new home—for now.

31

If Sadness Was Snow

Zenica, Bosnia and Herzegovina – Mid-December 1994

Winter. Snow outside. Sorrow inside. Our shelter—a former day-care—is packed with refugees from all over Bosnia and Herzegovina. Homeless. Malnourished. Traumatized. If the sadness was snow—it would melt. But it isn't and it doesn't. It stays like a permanent marker.

At least we're not alone. We share our sorrow with others—refugees from Prijedor, Kozarac, Maglaj, Doboj, Sanski Most, Banja Luka, Bosanski Novi and Srebrenica. Places I've only heard of. People who lost as much as we did—and more.

Their loved ones were killed. Burned. Beaten. Forced into camps like Manjača, Omarska, Keraterm, Trnopolje. Some talk about it. Others don't. Their bodies do.

At first, I just listen. Watch. It helps not to think about how I feel. But the more I listen, the more I care. These strangers grow on me. Their pain becomes mine.

Unlike snow, my sadness doesn't melt. It grows. My tears freeze it into ice.

Mama notices. She doesn't say anything. But when someone starts telling their story, she changes the subject or tells me to take a walk.

We're safe from bombs now. Most days, we eat. We're free. I should be happy. But I'm not. Any sudden sound— a voice, a noise—makes me jump. Makes me feel back there. Hiding. Running.

My heart races. Breathing gets hard. I can't swallow. And sometimes, I think I'll choke on air.

The lines here are long—just like they were at the barbed wire place. There's a line for the bathroom. A line for food. A line for the cold-water shower.

Once in a while, we get a bar of soap and a tiny bottle of shampoo we save. But there's no warm water. No heat. No electricity. No television. No radio.

Just a candle—used only when light is absolutely necessary. Like going to the bathroom at night.

Just like in the Nova Trgovina Camp, Hangari. Just like in Vranduk. Showers are rare.

By now, I'm used to the smell. It doesn't bother me anymore. It's familiar.

Each person's smell tells a story—of loss, of tragedy, of survival, and a pinch of hope hanging by a thread, like a loose tooth.

One day, there was no food. Nothing at all. My stomach grumbled louder than ever, a deep ache that felt like tiny claws scratching inside me. My head spun, and everything got blurry like I was underwater. I tried to stand, but my legs wouldn't hold me.

I fell down hard, my cheek scraping the cold floor. The world tilted, colors faded, and the hungry growls inside me got so loud they drowned out everything else. My throat felt dry and tight, like I was swallowing sand.

Ari sat nearby, staring off like she didn't care, lost in her own world. Mama had secretly given her a salty cracker when she cried earlier. Ari held it tight, pretending it was enough. But when I fainted, her eyes widened. Suddenly, she knew she wasn't the only one starving.

"Mama!" I heard someone shout. My ears buzzed, and I couldn't open my eyes.

Mama was there, her face pale and worried. She cupped my cheek and whispered, "Stay with me, sweetie. Don't go."

Now I'm a sweetie who passed out. Mama almost lost me. Maybe those American TV shows she watches are rubbing off on her, with all their dramatic catchphrases.

I wanted to cry but I was too weak. The hunger was heavy in my chest, a wildfire that wouldn't go out.

Mama's hands shook as she held me. I felt her breath on my forehead, warm and scared. She rocked me gently like I was a baby again.

That day, I understood hunger wasn't just an empty belly. It was a loud, painful monster that made me small and scared.

After a long time, I woke up to the smell of bread. We got breakfast and a late lunch.

On the nights when hunger gnaws too loud, we leave the shelter and stand in line outside the military barracks for their leftovers.

Most nights, we don't even know what we're eating—only that we're eating.

32

Dervish and Aldi

Zenica, Bosnia and Herzegovina – January 1994

The city feels like a tired heart—still beating, but barely. Zenica, once full of smoke from Željezara factory chimneys and music spilling from cafés, now breathes in whispers. In winter, the snow covers everything—bombed-out buildings, broken roads, even memories. It doesn't feel like it's falling from the sky anymore. It just lingers. Heavy. Reluctant. Like the people.

The walls of our shelter—a former daycare are painted with faded rainbows and cartoon suns, peeling behind our beds—if you can call mattresses on the floor "beds." Each morning, we wake up colder than the night before, wrapped in borrowed blankets that smell like strangers.

Outside, Zenica is both quieter and louder than I remember. There are no car horns, no children playing, no street musicians. But there are sirens. Shouts. Every sudden sound sends a ripple through my spine. My body remembers even when my mind tries to forget.

The soldiers on the street look older than us but younger than Mama. Some have frostbite on their fingers. Some don't even wear gloves. They check papers. Sometimes they hand out bread. Sometimes, they just stare.

Then, the snow melts. Slowly. Cautiously. Like it doesn't trust the warmth.

Some days, we go to school. Other days, we stay in the shelter. I borrow books from my Serb teacher—the one who stayed with his people: Bosniaks, Croats, Serbs. Those who refused to hate. Who stood against the war. Against genocide. On days without school, I read. And I write. Nana once told me about the book *Dervish and Death*. She even said that some believe it might be based on the life of Ilhamija, a poet and dervish from our hometown. That's why I pick it. I found it on a dusty shelf in our Zenica daycare refugee shelter library. I read *Derviš i smrt* by Meša Selimović because, like the main character Ahmed Nurudin, I too live in a cruel, immoral time. I read by the flicker of rationed candlelight, my jacket still on, socks stiff from cold. I don't understand every word, but I understand enough. The silence in the book sounds like the silence in our shelter—the kind that suffocates, the kind that watches you cry and doesn't move.

The dervish, Ahmed Nurudin, lost his brother. He tries to save his brother, but he loses himself. Nana said that Ilhamija's Path was similar. He searched for justice—and found only fear.

In our shelter, I listen to stories—of men taken and never seen again. Of neighbors who became guards. Of screams that follow you, even after you leave the camps. There is no justice here. Only waiting. Only hunger.

Only the sound of babies crying, mothers rocking them to sleep, elderly coughing, and quiet sobs that never stop. The dervish tried to reason with the world. So do we.

I feel like the dervishes in the books.

Sometimes, I think I lose myself too.

The innocent old Aldi—the one I miss so much—

I wish I could be like her, like she died inside but was free.

But this new me, Aldi, she's alive on the outside.

But inside, she's lost, broken, and weak.

The people with power—they are cruel.

They don't care about us, not now, not back then.

They make rules that hurt people.

They watch us suffer and don't help.

Why do they have so much and we have so little?

Why do they forget we are human too?

Why does my heart feel so heavy?

Why do I feel so tired even when I'm awake?

Can someone help me find the old Aldi again?

Or am I lost forever?

We stand in line and ask for food like it's supposed to come just because we need it. We tell ourselves this will end. That spring means something.

But snow melts. Sorrow doesn't. Fear doesn't. Flashbacks tire my eyes.

Mama says I'm too young for such a book. Maybe she's right. What if she's wrong? The war changed me. This isn't the old me. I'm no longer a child. I've been robbed of my childhood. War is difficult—reading books isn't. I'm not too young for books—only for wars.

I think I understand something the wandering dervish never did...you don't need to become cruel to survive cruelty. You just need to remember.

And write it down.

33

The Body Remembers

Zenica, Bosnia and Herzegovina – February 1994

S pring came, but not for us. The snow has melted. It's gone. Our sadness isn't. It stays—frozen in eternity.

We have a radio now. Some days, we even have electricity. When it works, I press my ear close and listen to the news. Hoping to hear that Tata isn't dead. Waiting for—something. Anything.

Grass pokes through the ice like it's afraid it might be punished for trying. Just like us—hesitant, unsure, fragile. A few trees bloom too early. Kind of like me. The petals don't last. But the air changes. It carries smells again—not just smoke and rot, but something else. Something like life.

Somewhere in America, someone is eating McDonalds. Somewhere, in Australia, someone is playing a guitar. Somewhere, in Hawaii, someone breaks out in laugher—brief, but real.

An unexpected touch. A glass shattering. A child popping a balloon. A dog barking. A toilet flushing.

That's all it takes. And the body remembers.

I don't know how much longer I can do this. I'm tired all the time.

On days when there's no school, all I do is sleep and eat the little food we're given.

Lately, I don't feel like reading. My brain is tired and reading is starting to make it worse. I don't feel like writing either. Nothing brings me joy anymore.

I can't finish the food, so I give mine to Ari.

The bread tastes like dust. Sometimes I chew and chew, but I still can't swallow. My clothes hang loose. My chubby cheeks have sunk—like the Titanic, swallowed by the ocean of war.

Only two weeks ago, I was out there. On the streets. Selling soap, conditioner and other hygiene products.

My dimples are gone now—hiding, like we did in Žepče, just before we turned ourselves in and were taken to camp. Like I'm doing it now. Refusing to get out. To go on.

Even when we have warm water, I don't want to shower. I'd rather lie in my own sweat.

It makes me feel like I'm the one in charge—like, for once, I get to decide what happens to my body, not someone else.

Every now and then, we get electricity. The moment the lights come on, it's like a hope bulb shining—warming our faces, making people smile. Even for a moment, it feels like something good is coming.

I can see hope in tired, hungry, afraid faces—but not in my own.

The other day, I looked in the mirror.

This wasn't me. Not the old Aldijana from before the war. I thought maybe I'd see the old me. The girl from before the war. The girl who loved to get into fights and compete. The girl who climbed trees. The girl who believed her birthday would always come with cake.

But she's not there.

This new girl was different. Thin and silent, like she had already given up the fight.

Like she lost—and somehow, was okay with the defeat.

Like she was just waiting to be called to get on the bus—to wherever people go when they've stopped hoping.

This nine-year-old me looked more like a ninety-year-old who has seen, heard, smelled and tasted too much. Maybe not that old, but an old soul.

I can still see hope in other people's faces. Even the tired ones. The hungry ones. The ones who shake in their sleep. But not in mine.

I don't know where my hope went. Maybe it's hiding somewhere deep, like my dimples.

Or maybe I gave it away, piece by piece, like I did with my food.

And just when I accepted my fate—when I lay down, waiting for a slow, quiet death—God intervened.

He didn't speak through thunder or light. He sent a messenger.

It wasn't Moses. It wasn't Jesus. It wasn't Mohammed. Or an angel with wings. It was people in blue vests.Strangers—no longer bystanders—finally stepping into the blood-soaked silence of my Bosnia. My Herzegovina. UN High Commissioner for Refugees.

They came. They saw.

The brutalities of the stupidest war.

A war of neighbors. A war over names. Over flags. Over the way we pray. Or not pray. Like my father, who refuses to pick a side.

I still don't understand it. Grown-ups killing each other because of invisible lines. Because of what's in our heads. Or our hearts. What kind of war is that?

34

She Still Loves Him

Zenica, Bosnia and Herzegovina – March 1994

Now that the UNHCR is here, things are changing. For the better—they say.

It's been more than eight months since we left Žepče, our hometown.

Eight months without seeing my father. Without hearing his voice. Without smelling the wood on his skin—after long days of building stools, tables, windows...and whatever else people needed to make a life.

The smell of sawdust meant he was home. Now, I'd give anything just to smell it once more.

I'd even relive the day he cut his thumb on one of his machines—the way they wrapped it in a towel and rushed him to Zenica to try to stitch it back. Or the day he fell off the roof of Nana's ranch style home.

Just to see him. Just to hear his voice. Just to know he's real and not something my memory made up.

But the air here is different.

It smells like metal beds, boiled soup, dirty cloth diapers, throw up, pee, poop—and the clothes of too many people packed into one room.

The other day, Mama ran into this guy. Tall. And judging by Mama's face—handsome.

We were on our way to Mama's cousin's house to shower and maybe eat something. Out of nowhere, this dude stops us.

He looks at Mama the way Tata used to. Like she's the most beautiful woman in the world. Arijana and I just stand there. Watching. Confused. Uncomfortable. Angry.

They talk. They laugh. Mama says he's her ex-boyfriend. I hate him. I hate his nice smile. I hate his kind eyes.

"Leave my mom alone, you creep!" Ari and I yell at him.

He says, "Your mom is just an old friend. Nothing else."

He says it like he means it. But I don't trust him. Or his ex-ass.

I don't think I'll ever trust anyone again.

"Ari," I whisper later, "I'd rather have the Serbs and Croats shoot me than let another guy who's not Daddy talk to Mom—ever again."

Mama makes us take a shower, even though I fight her the whole way.

She says it's because we stink. But I know it's punishment—for yelling at her ex-boyfriend. I scrub my skin so hard it turns red. It bruises.

What if Tata doesn't make it? What if they beat him to death in some camp?

Will Mama date other men? Will she marry someone else?

I swear—if any man ever tries to take my father's place, I'll kill him with my own two hands. I don't care how kind his eyes are. There's only one man who belongs in our family. And he's not here.

We shower. We eat meat for the first time in months. Mama's cousins are nice. Too nice.

But why? What if they want to adopt one of us? Or both of us?

I don't really want their meat. Or their bread. But I eat anyway. Because I'm afraid. What if Mama thinks I'm ungrateful? What if she leaves us here—with them—and goes off with her ex-boyfriend? Maybe she already wants to. Maybe that's why she made us shower.

We spend the day at their beautiful house—just like ours once was. Nice furniture. A balcony. A big bathroom. Light pouring through clean windows. It's not fair. It's not fair that some people get to live in their homes and eat good food. It's not fair that some people get to be happy. It sucks. I hate it.

I hate the smell of their clean kitchen. I hate the way the lights work when you flip a switch. I hate that we're not the ones living here.

They talk. They tell jokes. They're funny. Once, I almost laughed too. But I stopped myself. How can we laugh—when Daddy is still in a concentration camp?

"Did you guys hear? Soon, you'll be able to visit Tata in Žepče," Mama's cousin says.

"What? Visit him? In the concentration camp?" Mama asks—surprised, smiling. Smiling. Alhamdulillah.

"She won't run off with her ex. She still loves Dad. She hasn't forgotten him," I tell Arijana all happy.

I exhale—slow, deep—like a heavy stone just rolled off my chest.

I can't believe it. I'll finally get to see him. But... what if he's different? What if I don't recognize him? What if he doesn't recognize me? What if he stopped loving us? What if the camp broke his mind, twisted his heart, erased the parts of him that were...Tata? What if the man we see only looks like him—but doesn't think like him, doesn't act like him, doesn't love like him?

What if the real Daddy is gone, and this is just his shadow? What if he drinks himself to death? Beats us up until we bleed? Cheats on Mama? Stops providing for us? And becomes a monster himself? What, then?

Just before night falls on what used to be smokey Zenica—we leave. The streets are quieter now. Colder. As we walk back to shelter, we make plans. We'll visit Father the day after tomorrow.

35

Fake Smiles

Žepče, Bosnia and Herzegovina – March 1994

Mama must've gotten her period—again. The last time she was this moody was back in concentration camp. Almost nine months ago.

I don't get it. She should be happy. Arijana is. I am too. I swear, if her ex has anything to do with her crankiness, I'm going to tell Tata to spray paint his stupid car. In big, red letters: Wife Thief.

The trains are working again! We take the train to Begov Han. Then we walk the rest of the way to Žepče.

Are we like Ilhamija from Žepče, the dervish and poet, my cityman, marching toward death with open eyes and quiet hearts? Ilhamija walked to his execution with his dervish poems in his pocket. Before he left, he wrote, "Kad dođe vrijeme, niko izbjeći ne može."

When the time comes, no one can escape it.I think about that all the time—life, death, and fate.

It's like even the brave get swallowed by silence. Even the Serbs and Croats can't outrun death.

Hahaha! Maybe they'll die one day too, just like everyone else!

121

Maybe even the people in power who think they're so important. I bet they don't have funny poems in their pockets, just big old worries.

That's the only kind of justice in this world, I guess.

Death doesn't care if you're a Serb, a Croat, or a dervish poet from my city. It's the great equalizer.

But what if the Croats tricked us? What if they want to hurt us?

What if Tata is gone? What if he's dead?

Why does this scary feeling sit so heavy in my chest?

Can someone hold me when I'm so scared?

Or do I have to be brave like Ilhamija even when I don't want to?

Hey, if you see the old Aldi, tell her I'm still looking, okay?

One of Mama's cousins—one of the lucky ones who escaped to Germany—sent us a package. Inside, I find the prettiest outfit I've seen in months: a gray tunic with pink stripes and matching bottoms. I put it on right away. Today is special. I even ask Mama if I can wear her red lipstick.She lets me. Surprisingly, she lets Arijana too.

For a moment, we feel like girls again—just girls. Not war girls. Not refugee girls. Just girls getting ready to see their dad. But then something changes in Mama's face. She picks up the lipstick. She wipes our mouths clean. No explanation. Just quiet hands and a tightened jaw. She even wipes off her own lipstick. Careful. Thorough. Like it never happened.

Like it might remind them. Like it reminded us— of those nights in that shithole camp, when the pretty girls got taken. The way the mothers cried. The way we all pretended not to hear. Like being clean, or happy, or hopeful might make us a target again. A rape target— whatever that means. *I think I know what it means.*

Surprisingly, we get to Žepče quickly. No delays. No soldiers. No yelling. We even feel... rested. Arijana runs ahead, her little legs moving fast, not once complaining that her feet hurt. Like for a moment, the war forgot about us. First, we stop by my mother's aunt's house. We eat beans and bread. Simple, but warm. And it fills more than just our stomachs. She used to be a schoolteacher—used to take me to her school. I was seven. That's when I knew that in addition to being an author, I wanted to be a teacher. Just like her.

She taught Bosniak kids. Serb kids. Croat kids. Now, the same kids—some of them soldiers—stand at checkpoints with guns. They forced her husband to crawl on his hands and feet. To oink like a pig. While they laughed. Spit on him. Called him names. Our captors—our beloved neighbors. Her ex-students.

We eat so fast. Our food barely chewed. Swallowed. Ready to visit Daddy. We are at the gate of the barbed wire place—not Hangari. Somewhere else. A young soldier, no older than seventeen, leads us inside. Stares at me like a hungry dog who hasn't eaten for days. My feet tremble, and my heart beats fast like a champion in a race. Mama notices and squeezes my hands tighter. She gives him that look that says, *You better not come any closer, beast.*

There are lots of wooden tables and chairs. Families sitting. Talking. Smiling. Crying. The Croats walk around, feeding their egos. Some, even smiling. Acting like heroes—as if giving us visitation rights makes them kind. Like we'll forget. Forget the camps. The hunger. The beatings. The humiliation. The corpse in Rijeka Bosna. The scavengers, feasting on it.

But I know better. It's only because of the UN.

36

Chocolate War

Zenica, Bosnia and Herzegovina – Mid-March 1994

We sit. And wait. Then sit and wait some more. Our feet won't stay still—shaking, bouncing—like maybe if we move fast enough, time will too. I pick at my split ends, separating strand by strand. Ari leans over and whispers something into Mama's ear. Mama just nods. She bites the skin around her nails, like it might give her the same kick she used to get from cigarettes.

Just as I'm about to stand up and stretch my legs—there he is. My father. Ari's dad. Mama's husband. I recognize him by his walk. He still walks the same way—head held high, proud, like an official wearing a badge of honor.

I want to run up to him. Throw my arms around him. Bury my face in his shirt and breathe in the sawdust. But I don't. The Croat guards with guns remind me that this is a concentration camp, not a playground. So, I stay seated. My knees bounce. My throat tightens. And I wait for him to come to us.

Mama holds Arijana in her lap, like she's afraid that if she doesn't—Ari will run to him. Like we'll forget the rules. Like love might get us in trouble. So we sit. Like good little war girls. Waiting for permission to feel.

A middle-aged armed guard with nerd glasses unties his hands and points him toward us. Then turns around, giving him permission to walk alone.

How much I missed that smile. That face. Those blue eyes—pausing on Ari first, then me, then Mama. Like he's trying to decide who needs him most. But only for a second. Then he opens his arms—and we all run. Like nothing else matters. All four of us—together—again. Even if just for a moment. We kiss and hug. And kiss and hug. Like never before.

Before we even sit down, Tata pulls a jar of Eurokrem, a white and black chocolate spread from his coat pocket. A whole jar of chocolate spread—just for us.

More sugar than the twenty-two of us had in Vranduk during those five months. Plus, the four months in Zenica. Nine months' worth of sugar. In one little jar. From one big heart. Not only do I get to see my dad, I also get to stuff myself with hazelnut chocolate.

We dip our fingers in, licking the sweetness slowly—like we can stretch this moment if we're careful enough. Mama and Tata talk. They have so much to say. So much to catch up on. I study him while they speak.

He looks like Amiđa Nurija now—same cough, same sickly color. Just skin and bones. But no bruises. His hair is combed. Beard brushed. Too neat. Too clean. Kind of creepy, actually. You'd think he was on some work trip. Not trapped behind barbed wire like an animal.

I imagined him all bruised up. Barely walking. Not talking. Like the walking dead. But he's sitting here. Upright. Smiling. Even cracking a joke or two.

I know it's just an act. The Croats are putting on a show—letting the world think they're human. Like they're decent. Like this place isn't a prison. Like our fathers aren't starving behind barbed wire.

They've cleaned him up. Gave him a comb. Maybe even a warning. Smile. Behave. Pretend. I know that underneath the baggy clothes, there are proofs. Marks of real torture—beating, punching, hitting, kicking, spitting.

Stories he'll never tell. Wounds he'll carry to his grave. Because that's him. Protecting us—from what his body, and soul, have had to survive. But his body is keeping score. Remembering.

37

Too Good to be True

Žepče, Bosnia and Herzegovina – Mid-March 1994

We kiss goodbye and leave—like it's any other day. Like, we're going to see each other again tonight. I still can't get over how good Father looked. How civil, the Croat guards were. It's like a dream, one masked with smiles stretched over monstrous faces.

We walk to my mother's aunt's once-beautiful, three-story home near the city center. It used to be white. Now it's gray. Still tall but slouched—like something is dragging it down. Walls pockmarked with holes. Windows stripped of glass, wrapped in plastic.

With the UNHCR watching and taking notes, they let the civilians go. Shut down the camps. Send civilians home. To house arrest. A long way from freedom. If questioned, they must tell a lie—say there were no civilian camps in Žepče.

That it was all just "temporary housing." That the barbed wire was for protection. That the guards were there to keep them safe.

Not to beat them. Starve them. Threaten to kill them if they stepped out of line. Not to make the men disappear at night—one by one—without explanation. Not to rape the pretty girls. They even made them memorize lines. "Everything is fine." "We were treated well." "There was enough food." But we all knew the truth. And so do they.

A moment ago, I was in chocolate heaven. Sugar high. Watching my Daddy. Hugging him. Kissing him. But now—I'm the saddest girl in the entire universe. Feeling worse now than before.

Worse than when I thought I'd never see him again. Because now I know what I'm missing. And I have to lose him all over again. Mama says she has a headache. Arijana licks chocolate off her fingers and takes another bite of bread. She sips the powdered milk from the UN box—the one that looks like milk but tastes like sadness. We all sit in silence. Then—a knock at the door. Someone gets up. Opens it.

"Otkud ti?" she asks, like she's seen a ghost. "Your loved one can spend the night," says the Croat we know.

"But tomorrow, he needs to return."

And just like that—there he is. Behind the wall of smoke. Father. A tiniest atom in me, believing in humanity.

38

Orphaned Dreams

Žepče, Bosnia and Herzegovina – Mid-March 1994

We stay up late, candles burning one after another. Upstairs, Ari and I talk, laugh, cry, and tell jokes, pretending the war never happened. It's like none of this ever did, like life is still going on the way it should have, could have, would have, if only the Serbs and Croats had listened with their hearts, not with ears full of greed and hate. If only their hungry bellies hadn't swallowed all that nationalistic nonsense.

Mama and Tata stay downstairs, talking quietly together. It's way past our bedtime, but someone has to watch Ari sleep. So, we go to the guest room that's upstairs—it has a wall full of books—poetry, history, fantasy, spirituality. They let me bring a candle to read by.

On the top shelf, two thick books stand side by side, a Quran and a Bible. The Torah rests next to them, sharing the same shelf. Quiet and peaceful, like they enjoy each other's company.

I've read parts of the Quran translation before, but I'd never opened the Bible until now. I flip through it, page by page, looking for something, something that says whether killing neighbors, brothers, and sisters is condemned or allowed in this book. No luck.

A loud noise bursts from outside. My heart jumps. I slide the Bible back next to the Quran, then hug Ari, close my eyes, and sleep.

I wake up to Father's soft kiss, his goodbye. In the strangest way, I feel hopeful.

"Take care of each other. I'll see you soon," he says as he leaves the room, blowing kisses.

Arijana cries. She doesn't want him to leave. Neither do I. But I understand that this must be. My crying won't make things better. It won't bring him back. If I want him back—I have to be brave. We eat a small breakfast and leave. Tetka packs a bag for us. We walk back to Begov Han.

Mama doesn't look like herself. She doesn't walk like herself. Even Arijana is faster. Mama keeps stopping—taking breaks, massaging her belly. The belly that used to be big and strong. Now just loose skin, hanging like an empty sack.

It's a surprisingly warm day for March. Warm—not hot. But Mama sweats. Each time she takes a break, she sits and hugs her bent legs, like she's trying to squeeze the pain out. I watch her. I don't say anything to Ari. Trying not to scare her when deep inside I'm terrified that she'll pass out and die.

Just before Begov Han, Mama collapses. Her body, still. Pale. Like she really is dead. We stand next to her, too afraid to touch her. A river of tears rolls down our faces. Our voices loud. Then louder. Loudest. Begging for help. Someone hears our cries. They run. And return—with help. An army paramedic, carrying a stretcher. They load Mama's still body onto it. Like she's already gone. Like they're taking her to be buried. I knew things were too good to be true. I knew we'd have to pay for it.

Ari won't stop crying. I can't either—but I try to stay quiet. Someone needs to stay strong. Even if it's just pretend. They let us walk beside the stretcher. One on each side. Like little soldiers. Like we're escorting something sacred.

A woman with a scarf covering her gray hair and wrinkles that don't belong to her young age takes us in. She gives us a sugar cube and water. She makes halva. The smell of melted flour, butter and sugar water calms me down. It brings me back to Nana Điha's house. It reminds me of Bajram, Kurbanski and Ramazanski.

Ari falls asleep on the couch, her thumb near her mouth. A crochet doily draped over the top of the coffee table like a crown—like even this battered house still believes in being royal.

I sit next to her, knees pulled to my chest, watching her breathe. Each inhale a tiny Bismillah. Each exhale, a quiet Amin.

I want to sleep too. But my brain won't shut off. What if Mama dies? What if we never go back? What if this is the part where everything falls apart? The grownups whisper in the kitchen.

"Keno is on his way."

I've been carrying war in my chest for months now. It's heavy—but it fits. I'm so lost in my head that I don't make a connection. Our Keno is on his way. Tetka Azra's son. Rahmetli, Tetak Ibrahim's oldest. Shot twice. Survived.

And suddenly the air feels thinner. Like the house itself remembers. Like it wants to cry, too. I glance at Ari—still asleep. And I think how lucky she is, to still have dreams. Because mine feel like an orphanage now. Fatherless. Motherless. Crowded with ghosts. And no one left to tuck them in.

39

If Only I Could Sleep

Begov Han, Bosnia and Herzegovina – Mid-March 1994

Keno takes us to the abandoned Serb home where they live now. Nana Điha, Tetka Azra, Fatima, Adem, Haris, and Jasmin wait inside.

It's foggy, and the air smells like burning wood, charcoal, plastic—whatever people can find to keep warm. My throat itches. I can't stop coughing.

As soon as we get in, I drink water. Ari runs off to play with Haris and Jasmin. I stay with Nana.

We don't talk. She just takes off her hijab— revealing sparkles of silver hair with the dark locks barley clinging on. She scratches her scalp and hands me a comb.

"Dijete drago, Bog ti dao svako dobro," she says again and again, asking God to reward me, as if plucking her gray hairs is some kind of sacred offering.

I sit down on what's supposed to be a couch, a wooden bed frame with two thin sponge pads, one to lean on, one to sit. And I begin pulling, one gray at a time.

I'm not gonna lie. It's satisfying for both of us. With each gray hair I pull, I feel lighter. And so does she.It's almost like Nana's grays are more than just hair—they're the unwanted things in both of our lives. Our losses. Our traumas. Our failures.

One by one, we pluck them away. Like maybe, if we keep going, we'll find a version of ourselves untouched by war.

I feel so out of it. I'm not mad. I'm not sad. No more tears to shed—only the invisible kind. The ones in my stomach. In my chest. In my head. The worst kind.

First, I lost my father. Now, I've lost my mother. And tomorrow—I'll lose my sister. Arijana is going to Zenica to stay with Mama's rich cousins. There isn't enough food for both of us. One extra mouth to feed is one too many. And there's no space, either.

We sleep on the cold floor of an unfinished Serb home. No plumbing. No heat. No water. No insulation. Just red brick walls, and the smell of cement and burning trash. Ari leaves. And I stay.

After she's gone, I curl up in one corner of the only room in the house—alone. In a fetal position, just like I did nine years ago inside Mama's belly.

My cousins try to talk to me, but I ignore them. There's nothing to say. I'm the world's biggest loser. And there's nothing more to lose. And strangely—I'm okay with it. I lie there and pray. I'm done with this stupid life. More than ever, I want to leave this world behind. I want to cross to the other side.

I've served my earthly hell sentence here. I want to go to heaven—and wait for the rest of my family to join me. I stop eating. Stop drinking. I don't need food. What I need is my family. That's all. I look outside. It's snowing.

Smoke rises from the chimneys. No living soul in sight. Only ghosts. Bosniaks. Serbs. Croats. All the ones killed—now holding hands, like they should have in life. Calling out to the people still here. Telling them to wake up. To stop. But no one listens.

The war is still very much alive. Out there. And in here. In this house. In every shelter and home. In my crazy head. And in the crazy heads of others. Different kinds of wars.

The snow stops. The sun peeks out, soft and slow, like it's not sure if it's welcome. It begins to melt the snow—drop by drop, bit by bit. I sit up and watch it melt, wishing that one day, my sorrow, my grief, my pain, my nightmares will melt away too. Perhaps then, I'll finally be able to close my eyes and rest in my sleep.

40

Bread for Mama

Begov Han, Bosnia and Herzegovina – Late March 1994

I'm still in Begov Han. Mama's still at the hospital in Zenica. And Father's still in the concentration camp. Nana forces me to eat. She spoon-feeds me, just like when I was little. At night, when everyone sleeps, I hear her sobbing. It breaks my heart. So, I eat. I think she sobs for me.

And slowly, I begin to feel again. Sad. Mad. I snap at my cousins. I give my aunts a hard time. But no one minds. They don't yell. They don't tell me to stop. It's almost like, they'd rather have me rude than broken.

I begin to eat. I even ask for seconds, though I never get them. But still, I ask. It's like the heavy, foggy cloud over my head has finally lifted. And the sun—is beginning to shine again. Once again, mess bothers me. So, I pick things up. I wipe. I sweep. I move things over—like this is my house and I get to decide where things go. I can tell it's driving Tetka Azra and Fatima nuts. But they let me.

They know how much I need this. They don't even say anything when I yell at my boy cousins for making a mess. And for whatever the reason—Jasmin, Haris and Adem seem chill. They let me act, but they don't react. It's their way of showing they care, silently. Without hugs and kisses. Just letting me be. Letting me exist.

They take me to visit Mama in the hospital. Arijana is there too. I'm not sure who to run to first. I wait. I contemplate. Mama just had surgery—so I pick her. We walk in. The hospital is full—of sick, the wounded, the malnutritioned. Of the emotionally broken. Young and old. With visible wounds. And invisible ones. Each wound—a tragic, traumatic story waiting to be told.

There are people with missing limbs. No ears. No eyes. People talking to the invisible ghosts. Arguing. Kicking. Screaming. Even fighting the ghosts. Fists in the air—battling memories no one else can see.

Tetka Fatima can't handle it. Her body goes into shock. She drops to the ground. Unconscious. Someone grabs Ari and takes her out. They let me stay. They let me see Mama. I kiss Mama. She returns my kisses. Tells me how much I've grown. How pretty I've become. She admires me with her autumn-like eyes.

Mama is hooked up to machines. A clear liquid drips into her veins through a rubber tube and a needle. Her face looks tired like she hasn't slept for days. She says something ruptured in her stomach. It bled. Doctors operated, but are keeping an eye on her. Should be getting out soon. No room for people like her that are no longer in critical condition.

I give her the bread I've been saving. My gift. To her. She needs it more than me. At first, she refuses—shaking her head, whispering no, over and over. But I insist. So, she takes it.

We leave to catch the train back to Begov Han. Arijana returns to Zenica.

41

Dad's Second Birthday

Begov Han, Bosnia and Herzegovina – March 31, 1994

I 'm so sick of lentils, beans and cabbage. That's all we eat. That's all
we've been eating for months. I keep myself busy. Cleaning. Writing.
Reading. Taking nature walks. I'm coming to accept things the way they
are. Trying to find the silver lining in all of this. At least, we're alive.
Separated—but alive. And soon, Mama will be out.

To our surprise, a message comes from Žepče: the concentration camps
are being shut down—an order from the UN. It's March 31st, 1994. Nine
months of concentration camp for Tata. We wait for him at the main road.
Someone brought a blanket, just in case he's cold. I brought my hope. I
didn't even know I still had some. No one talks. We just stare down the road
like it's a tunnel to another life. Wind blows. The trees shake. My hands are
ice. And then—we see someone. Thin. Pale. Shoulders hunched like he's
holding the sky on his back. Gray beard. Unkept. Outgrown curly hair,
covering his ears, like it's trying to muffle the world. Eyes sunken—tired,
but not blind. He sees everything. Feels too much. Walks like he's made
of paper and history. He limps a little. Drags one leg behind the other. His
clothes hang off him like they don't belong to him. Nana starts crying. My

heart punches my chest so hard I can barely breathe. Ari and I race to him. His eyes find us—slowly, like he's not sure if we're real. I scream, "Tata!"

Arijana's already in his arms. I wrap myself around them both. He smells like metal and dust and something I can't name—but I don't care. He's warm. He's real. He's here. But I still don't believe it. It feels like I'm dreaming. What if I wake up—and he's gone?

I think of Mama. *What would she do if she were here instead of in the hospital? Would she run faster than us? Would she faint? Cry? Yell? Would she kiss his face a million times? Would she kiss his mouth, like they do in movies? Yuck! Maybe all of it. I miss her so much. What if she doesn't get better? What if I lose her? Will her life be the price I pay for getting him back?*

Why can't I just enjoy this moment? Stop catastrophizing, I tell myself.

I wish my brain had an off switch—just something I could flip to make it stop spinning, stop worrying. Nothing will ever be perfect. Life isn't a Hollywood movie or a romance novel. It never will be. So, I just hold on. Like if I let go—he might disappear again. But he doesn't. Not this time. It's him. It's Daddy.

And there's so much to celebrate. My father's second birthday.

42

His Golden Hands

Vranduk, Bosnia and Herzegovina – April 1994-June 1995

Nana hasn't missed a single salah. She's always up before sunrise to pray Fajr. At noon, she lays out her prayer mat and prays Dhuhr. In the afternoon, Asr. At sunset, Maghrib. And every night, before she goes to sleep, she prays Isha. She recites words in a language I don't understand—Arabic. Sometimes, I slip on my long-sleeve dress, the one that falls to my ankles. I cover my head with one of her scarves and follow along. I don't know the exact words she's saying, not all of them. So, I whisper the little I do know. It makes me feel grateful. At peace.

Before Mama came home from the hospital, I wrote her a little note and gave it to one of our relatives who went to Zenica to run an errand. They promised to drop it off at the hospital for me. The note said: *"Mama, Tata is coming home soon. We are all waiting for you. I love you."* I hope it made her smile. Daddy, Ari, and I clean the old house that belonged to Tetak's late grandmother—the one we're moving into. It's dusty, creaky, and gives me goosebumps, like her spirit never left. It feels haunted, like she's still there, watching.

I don't know what's worse—this creepy house, or going back to the old daycare center packed with refugees. We pick up Mama from the hospital in Zenica and head to Vranduk. Tata can't believe how much weight she's lost. He keeps staring at her, like people do when they're falling in love. She stares back. And then they smile at each other, like they can't get enough.

It makes me feel weird. Ari doesn't seem to care. She's too young to know about things like this. I've never seen them like this before—Mama and Tata. Not like this. When they think we're not looking, they hold hands. Like people in love do in the movies. I bet when we sleep, all they do is kiss. Maybe even on the mouth. Yuck!

The home is falling apart. The mud packed into the walls is starting to show, and the smell of mold feels permanent—like it's tattooed into the air. The old windows, from a time when boys stood outside and girls whispered to them from behind the glass, don't keep out the cold anymore. Most of the rooms aren't safe to live in. Father fixes up one room—just one—for all four of us. It's where we sit, eat, cook, sleep, go to the bathroom, and even bathe. Four of us, crammed into one small space. During warm weather, we use the outhouse to shower and go. But once the cold air comes, we pee and poop in a plastic bucket. We bathe in a baby-sized plastic tub. Tata built us something to sit and sleep on with little wood he collected from a nearby forest.

A traditional Turkish-style red rug covers the cold floor, its faded patterns trying to warm more than just our feet. We no longer starve. We ate meat at least once a week. Lots of potatoes, rice, flour, maslenica and veggie stews. For Eid, we even had sarma, burek, baklava and hurmašice.

Thanks to Tata's golden hands, life almost feels normal. We're still refugees living in a one room home, but we're together. And alive. That's all that matters. He gets a job in Golubinja, in a carpenter's shop. Our new neighbors give us a piece of land. We grow our own potatoes, onions, beans, peppers, cucumbers and tomatoes.

43

Srebrenica

Vranduk, Bosnia and Herzegovina – July 1995

It's July. Two months ago—I celebrated my eleventh birthday. Mama made baklava with a handful of nuts my sister and I stole from the neighbor's yard. We each got a tiny diamond piece of it. With my wet tongue, I lick my lips over and over even after the sweetness is gone. Mama let me make a wish into her green cigarette lighter. I wished for war to end.

We're no longer the only refugees in Vranduk. As selfish as it may seem, this makes me feel hopeful. Hopeful that perhaps someone might understand. And that villagers will forget our lice and scabies. They'll have someone else to pity—and to give sadaqa to.

Everywhere I look, women, children, and elderly are shaking their heads. An ocean of tears.

Srebrenica, Bosnia and Herzegovina: Eight thousand innocent Bosniak Muslim lives. Men. Women. And children. All killed horrendously by their neighbors. And their so-called leader—General Ratko Mladić.

A genocide. Committed against my people. For bowing their heads to Allah. One God. For all. The same God who made Adam. Abraham. Moses. Jesus. Mohammed. The messengers. Peace be upon them all. Jews. Christians. Muslims. Different. But the same. Too many graves.

I don't exactly know where Srebrenica is in Bosnia and Herzegovina. But I hope it's far from here.

I picture it as Srebreni Grad, a Silver City—with silver homes, buildings, people, food, mountains, trees, and farms all covered in precious metal like some sort of royalty.

The grown-ups say the word "genocide." I don't really know what it means. They say it means many people get hurt or killed just because of who they are. Like because of their religion or where they come from. It's like a big, mean bully who wants to hurt everyone in your group. That is why the grown-ups look sad and scared. Mama stands still. She holds her face and shakes quietly. I see her shoulders go up and down slowly. The room feels heavy and cold, even though the sun is shining a little. My throat feels tight. My stomach twists, but not in a good way. I wonder why someone would be so mean. I wonder if someone can stop it. I think about if my family will be safe. Maybe that's why Mama is so sad. The room is very quiet. I hear a clock tick and birds outside. It feels like we are all holding our breath. It's okay to feel scared and confused. I try to hope things will get better. I squeeze my hands tightly. They feel warm. "Srebrenica," someone says again.

Like saying it more will change what happened. Eight thousand. Eight thousand people. That's like—four thousand of me. And four thousand of Ari. And then more. Gone.

Just...disappeared from the world. Like they never even happened. I don't understand how that's possible. How do neighbors do that? How do people smile at you one day and kill you the next? How do they look at your baby and still pull the trigger?

I keep thinking maybe someone counted wrong. Maybe it's not eight thousand. Maybe it's a mistake. Maybe it's a lie. But no one's saying it's a lie. They're just crying. And so are we. Ari. Mama. And me. Crying like we'll never stop.

Mama finally lowers her hands. Her eyes are red. She looks at me like she's seeing something else behind my face.

"Could've been us," she whispers.

I want to say no. But I know she's right. It could've been us. It still could be.

I grab Arijana's hand and squeeze it tight. She squeezes back.

Then I close my eyes and imagine my silver city again—Srebrenica—Srebreni Grad. But now the silver is dripping red.

"They lined them up," a handicapped man nearby says. His voice sounds like gravel.

"Shot them like broken toys someone didn't want anymore. Buried them in holes. Then dug them up again. Broke their bones and hid them somewhere else."

I don't want to hear it. But I can't not hear it. My fingers shoved in my ears don't help. *What if we hadn't escaped? Would we be in one of those holes? Would Arijana?* I squeeze her hand.

She's not coughing anymore. She's just looking at me with wide eyes. Like maybe she heard it too.

"I'm scared," she whispers. "Me too," I say.

Then I try to smile. "But we're not in Srebrenica." She doesn't smile back.

44

What if She Dies?

Vranduk, Bosnia and Herzegovina – July 1995-May 1998

Mama is in and out of the hospital. Surgery after surgery. Bottles of medicine, neatly stacked on the top kitchen shelf—so we can't reach them. Each time she goes, they give her a new diagnosis. I worry she'll die. Sometimes, I even imagine it. Her body, lying still. The silence in the house. Our television, covered with a white bedsheet to respect the dead. Majka Zulka in the kitchen, hammering down the meat. Dido Hašim outside, fire spilling from his workshop. Father kissing another woman. And Ari and I—living on different continents, with our new families. How nothing would ever be the same. And then I cry into my pillow so no one hears.

After fourth grade, we go to school in Nemila. Sometimes, we have a bus. Sometimes, we don't—so we walk. We walk through two dark tunnels. No lights. Only walls. We carry a stick to guide us, tapping as we go so we don't get run over by the few cars that pass. I get good grades, and so does Ari. But mine have to be perfect. If they're not, I get so mad at myself.

Mama and Tata smoke a lot. So do their guests. It burns my throat and makes me cough, but I don't say anything. I don't want to ruin their honeymoon days. Once, my teacher accused me of smoking. Mama had to come to school to explain why I smell like a chimney.

Tata drinks every night, but I never see him drunk. Except for one time when they found him passed out near the road in the ditches. When he doesn't drink, he has that look in his eyes, the kind people have in scary movies. So, I don't mind when he drinks. That's when he almost seems happy. That's when I hear him sing and laugh, like before. Mama says he's not an alcoholic. Because when he drinks, he doesn't yell. He doesn't hit. I want to believe her. But I can't. I'm afraid that one day he may start yelling and hitting. Once, I dipped my finger in his glass. It was the most disgusting thing I ever tasted. Made my whole-body jump. Gave me goosebumps. That's when I knew—he drinks to forget. It's like his medicine. Why can't he just take aspirin like Mama, Ari, and me? I told him that once. He just turned his head and said nothing. He never talks about the concentration camps. I don't know if he got beat. But he talks about how he beat tuberculosis. How tuberculosis couldn't beat him—like it got Amiđa Nurija.

After the honeymoon phase, Mama and Tata fight a lot. And I don't understand why. It's like the smallest, stupidest thing turns into a trigger. Then one of them—or both—explode. When that happens, I take Ari out. I read to her. And I write. Little poems that rhyme. Then I read them to her. Except she never really listens. She just pretends. No one understands me. I don't even think I understand myself.

I have so much to process. To share. To write about. But I can't. Each time I sit and think about the war, I get migraines. I get sad. It's like I'm back there—again. Then I can't sleep. I can't eat. And I dream about dead people. Dead animals. Soldiers. Guns. Bombs. Snipers. Food. Moving. Being an orphan. Being homeless.

And the worst part is—my sadness never melts. It lives inside me, day and night. Like I'm possessed. It never lets me rest. It makes me envy the dead. It makes me tired all the time. If only I could rest when I sleep, maybe the sadness would melt away. A little sound continues to make my heart jump out of my chest. Crying becomes painful. So, I avoid it for as long as I can. Until it comes out like an explosion in my neck and chest. Not letting me breathe. Suffocating me. Like a rope tied around my neck, and a giant tank sitting on my chest.

School has become the only place where I feel like my old self. Being around family and their moods scares me. It's like walking on nails. I worry that any little mistake I make will tickle the monsters in their bellies and make them scream. The monsters made by war. So, I stay at school. Or at my friends' houses.

Once, I got physical with one of my friends. For no reason. One moment we were all laughing. Next, I was wrestling her on the ground. Her mother got upset and told us we deserved to be refugees. Because of the way we act. Because Father drinks. Because Mother doesn't wear a hijab. Because we don't go to mosques, like they do. She never says the other things out loud—but I can tell. I can feel them.

So, I decide to prove her wrong. Ari and I start going to Islamic School on the weekends. I learn about Islam. I learn surahs and duas. I learn how to pray—just like Nana Điha—in Arabic. I even learn Arabic letters. Begin to read the Qur'an. I prove her wrong. I prove them all wrong. We do belong—no matter what our names are. No matter where we come from.

No matter how, when, if or where we pray. Nobody deserves war. And for the first time in a long, long time...I feel like a winner. And I don't hate. I'm grateful.

45

When All This Becomes Yesterday

Žepče, Bosnia and Herzegovina – May-September 1998

We came back home. Our house—the one in Žepče, with the address B. 44. It's been three years since the Dayton Peace Agreement was signed. My country is now divided—into the Federation and Republika Srpska.

Coming home was all I dreamed of for five years. But now that we're back, it doesn't feel like my dreams. Our house looks the same as before the war—but it isn't. Because we are not the same either. And nothing will ever be the same again. There's no furniture. The car—gone. Only empty walls remain. Just like us. Empty. Walls that remember fear. Sorrow. Loss. Walls that echo with the sobs of the living—and the silence of those who never came back.

Everywhere I look, I see ruins. At first, still. Then moving—like a film that plays over and over. A film I don't want to watch anymore, but I can't turn it off. The sorrow stays. It seeps into my bones. Traps me in the past. I fight—I try to break free. I imagine that I am dead. I envy the dead. Because it's easier for them than for the lost. To lose yourself—that's how I feel. Too tired, like my old nana. Too young to fight the sorrow disguised as an evil witch. That's why I lose. I lose myself. Every time. But I keep fighting. Because maybe—one day—I will win.

I celebrated my fourteenth birthday with my friends in Vranduk—a place that isn't my home, but feels more like it now. Mama even got me a candle. I blew it out. I wished to return home. A month later, my wish came true. But now I wish it hadn't. Because the house where I was born no longer feels like home. Neither does Vranduk. Nor Zenica. And so I wonder—where is home? Will I ever find it? What if I don't? Will I always be a homeless dreamer, searching for a home with beautiful dreams—and not the bad ones? The ones that wake me. That make me sweat. That never let me forget.

Since Tata got out, we've been going to Split in Croatia all the time. Our trips are long and secret. Mama and Tata say we can't tell anyone. "Not a living soul," Mama whispers. "If anyone asks, our permanent address is in Split," Tata adds.

It feels like a secret mission. Like something terrible will happen if we say too much. So, I lie—the thing I hate most. We smile. We nod. Interview after interview at the American Embassy. Medical exams. Physicals. We pass. But deep down, I'm certain none of us would pass a mental test. I'm convinced we're all damaged. Especially me—because when I fall into that black hole, I envy the dead.

"If they ask for your address, say we're Bosnian refugees in Split," Tata says.

We do what our parents tell us. But my heart is split in two. Tata and Ari want to go to Chicago. I just want a quiet, safe home. Whenever we come to Split, I sleep like a baby. No sweating. No nightmares. Dry hands. Normal pulse. I dream of Chicago—far from Žepče. Srebrenica. Bosnia and Herzegovina. The broken Yugoslavia. And then—on the same day we return to the house in Žepče, a letter arrives. Stamped. Sealed. Approved. We're going to Chicago. As refugees. Just like that—everything changes. Hope pushes through the cracks of our broken walls. The future that once felt impossible now seems real. Possible. Close. But with hope comes sadness, guilt, and fear. And the sharp anxiety of the unknown. *What will life be like on the other side of the Atlantic? Will we fit in? Will we be welcomed? Will I understand the language, the culture, the people? Will we ever come back? Will this be the last time I see this street, this sky, this house?*

I'm excited. Afraid. I want to go. I want to stay. My chest is full of something heavy and light at the same time. Because starting over sounds beautiful... And impossible. But still, we're going. And maybe, just maybe—this time we'll be safe.

PART TWO: Take Me to America

46

When the Heart Carries Two Worlds

Žepče, Vranduk – September 1998

I lose track of how many times we've had to pack and unpack. Tata sells our green VW station wagon. That's all the money we have left.

It doesn't seem like enough. Hopefully, it'll be enough to get us to Chicago.

"You can stop by Dragana, Ljuba, and Ruža's house to see them one last time," Mama says—but there's a warning in her voice. "Make sure you don't tell them this is goodbye," she adds sharply. "They must not know we're going to America."

I nod, my stomach sinking. We became close. Muslim sisters with Catholic sisters. In a country where such friendship is forbidden.

But then Mama lowers her voice and points her finger like a blade, "I know they are your friends. But they are also Croats. And we must never, ever trust Croats from Bosnia."

Her words stay in the air, heavy and sharp. I want to say something. *I want to ask—what about before the war? When we laughed together? Shared sweets? Held hands and jumped rope?* But I don't. Because I know better. I nod, even though my chest tightens.

Mama's words echo: *Never, ever trust Croats from Bosnia.*

But what about the Croats from Split? The ones who welcomed us into their home like family? Fed us, gave us warm beds, let us live in their home? If it weren't for them, we wouldn't even have a chance at Chicago. Are they different? Or are we just pretending they are? What makes a Croat from Bosnia dangerous? But a Croat from Croatia safe?

I don't understand. I want to ask. But I'm scared she'll yell, or worse. So, I keep quiet. Instead, I nod again.

Because that's what we're supposed to do now. Nod. Smile. Lie to our friends. Leave without a goodbye. Because we're different.

Some of my friends have already kissed. Not me.

A blond boy I have a crush on asks me for a walk.

His name is Kenan.

He leads me behind the fortress, and we climb into a horse carriage that's been parked there forever.

He looks at me with his seductive green eyes—like the boys in American movies do when they're about to kiss the girl.

My heart races. I can't lie to myself—I liked it. I imagine myself as Kate kissing Leo in Titanic.

My hands are sweaty. So, this is what it must feel like. It's weightless, dreamy. Like if I spread my arms, I could fly.

I feel awkward and unsure, but I try to act cool. Somewhere in the distance, a dog barks. We pull apart.

He doesn't know I've never kissed anyone before.

"Aldijana," he says, leaning in, "I don't know if you realize how beautiful you are. I feel like this is all a dream—the best dream I've ever had. You're the most gorgeous girl I've ever seen."

Bullshit! I think. I don't want to wake up.

I want to believe him. But I don't see it. "Here," Kenan says, taking off a golden letter "K" pendant from his chain. I feel average. "Take this, so that I can always be with you. So that you never forget me."

I'm afraid that he's telling me what he tells every single girl he wants to kiss. "No, no, no. I can't take this," I whisper, panicking.

I bet it works each time. Not because I don't want it. But because if Mama or Tata find out, I won't need to punish myself alone anymore.

Because it works for me.

Then—he kisses me. "I won't leave you alone until you take it. Please. Do it for me."

His big lips press gently against mine. "Fine," I say, realizing how rude I sound. I kiss him back, but the whole time, I'm terrified someone might see us.

What if Tata finds out? Or Mama? They'll kill me with their bare hands. This carriage will be the last thing my eyes ever see.

"Thank you," I add, walking away, heart pounding. Minutes ago, I could fly. Now, my wings feel broken. *I hate my father and my sister! Why do we have to listen to them? Why do we have to go to stupid America now? It's not fair that two of them always get what they want.*

I'm so pissed, the sky begins to thunder. Rain crashes down on the macadam road. I run to Tetka Besima's house, salty tears mixing with the metallic rain.

That night, I stay up and write a poem. The next morning, we leave for Sarajevo. Another secret this Bosnian must keep.

47

Ready or Not, Here We Come

Žepče, Vranduk – September 1998

A do and Edo's dad, my uncle Nurija, died last winter. From tuber-culosis. From malnutrition, beatings, torture, trauma, and invisible mental illness that killed him. That day, Tata cried like a baby. Everyone cried. But not me. I had no tears. I was sad but couldn't cry. I kept asking myself why.

We took the rundown train—the very same uncle Nurija got off when they freed him from the concentration camp. He's gone now, buried in Žepče.

I whisper to Ari, "Do you think Edo and Ado wish they had what we have?"

She shrugs, her eyes distant.

"Maybe…. Our Tata is still alive. He's taking us far away. To a place of dreams. American dreams."

Life is funny like that. Sometimes others have things we wish for, and other times we have things they wish for. Yes, uncle got out earlier, but he died earlier. Tata stayed in the concentration camp longer, but he lived longer. I can only imagine how Edo and Ado feel.

I nod but the knot in my stomach tightens. "I don't know if I want to go," I admit.

Arijana looks at me, surprised. "You like Kenan, don't you?"

I glance away, cheeks burning. "Yeah. But what if everything changes? What if I lose this part of me—the part that's still just a kid?"

Tata calls from Tetka's yard, "Girls, come sit. We're about to leave."

I take a deep breath, trying to push down the fear. "You know, before all this, I used to be jealous of Arnela—her clothes, her hair, how everyone liked her. I bet she's probably jealous of me now," I smirk. "I mean, karma's funny like that. Maybe she wishes Kenan gives her a kiss, too."

Arijana giggles. "Yeah, like, 'Why did Aldijana get to kiss Kenan and not me?'"

I laugh, feeling lighter for a moment. "Exactly. Life's got jokes, even when it feels like everything's falling apart."

First, we board a tiny propeller plane—the kind that looks like it's already crashed a few times and just got patched up with duct tape and prayers.

I'm convinced we'll fall from the sky. It's my first time flying, and I'm nauseous with terror. My hands are cold and clammy. My chest tightens.

It's the same feeling I had during the war—like death is right around the corner, waiting to pounce.

No snacks. No drinks. No smiles. Just silence and scared Bosniak refugee faces, packed in tight, flying into the unknown. Flying into the diaspora.

We land in Dubrovnik, Croatia. Then Zagreb.

We board another plane—this one feels less like a metal coffin with wings. It takes us to LaGuardia Airport in New York.

From there, one last flight. LaGuardia to O'Hare, Chicago. I hold onto a pink teddy bear we bought at the pijaca in Sarajevo. It looks just like the one Mama snatched from my hands the day we walked toward the barbed wires—toward the concentration camp.

The one I had to leave behind. This time, no one's taking it from me. I squeeze it tight against my chest, like it can protect me from everything that's still ahead—the strange language, the cold streets, the loneliness, the memories. Maybe it can't. But maybe I don't need it to. Maybe I just need to remember: I made it here. And maybe—just maybe—this time I'll keep:

My sanity.

My health.

A new school.

A new country.

A new life.

An address.

Friends.

Love.

Myself.

Still scared.

But finally safe.

America—ready or not...here we come.

48

Books and Looks

Chicago, United States of America – September 1998

American airports look exactly like they do in Home Alone. Big. Loud. Flashing lights. People sprinting like Olympic athletes with roller bags.

Everyone's in a rush, but no one knows where they're going. It smells like French fries, anxiety, and overpriced perfume.

We land at O'Hare, and everything is huge and terrifying. I grip Mama's sleeve like a toddler.

"Mama, what if we get lost?" I whisper.

"We already are," she mutters, looking around nervously. "This place is a damn city."

Suddenly, we spot them—Mama's cousins, holding up a sign welcoming us like we're celebrities:

DOBRO NAM DOŠLI.

Some of the faces I recognize. Others—I just pretend I do. One woman hugs me so tight I think my spine cracks.

"Sječaš li se ti mene? Do you remember me?" she says, grinning.

"Umm... naravno," I lie, smiling.

"Of course she does," Mama answers for me, like she's afraid I'll say the wrong thing and offend someone before we've even unpacked.

Mama has a tendency to answer for me. It drives me nuts. I hate when she does that.

I rather mess up, and learn from my mistakes. I don't think she's aware of what she does. I don't think she knows that I hate when she talks about me and answers for me in front of others. It makes me feel slow. And I know I'm not dumb.

We pile into a huge van that smells like garlic and car freshener, and head to mother's aunt's house.

As soon as we walk in, the smell of Bosnian food hits me like a warm, meaty hug. Sarma, pita, begova čorba, hurmašice. I don't know whether to cry or eat everything.

"Sit, sit! You're too skinny! You look like war!" someone yells as they shove food onto my plate.

Everyone's happy—loud, laughing, showing off their broken English like it's a trophy.

"Dis is my cous' from Bosna," one cousin announces proudly.

"She survived war. Very smart. Strong like Amer'kan woman!"

"I hef... two jobs," another cousin adds with a flip of her hair like she's Oprah. "I buy new tools from Hondipo"

We stay for about a week. Every day, it's a new errand.

"Tomorrow, we go Soshal," Tata says one night while peeling an orange with a knife like it's war ration.

"You mean Soshal Sekyurti Ofis," Mama corrects.

"Den Pablik Ed. You nid say rait. Amerikans lav wen immigrants spik korekt Amerikan Inglish."

Ari and I burst into laughter. They're so funny when they try to speak English.

Next day: Social Security cards. Then the Department of Human Services, which everyone calls "Public Aid," even though it sounds like a line for free soup and judgment.

People stare at us like we're aliens with bad fashion. People of all colors and shapes of eyes.

After that, we visit our soon-to-be cockroach kingdom: a tiny, dusty apartment on Wallen Street in Rogers Park. Third floor. No elevator. One bedroom. Old carpet. A smell I can't quite describe—like socks and sadness.

"This will be home now," Mama says, trying to sound excited. Ari looks around and whispers, "Home for who? The rats?"

Then school decisions. Ari gets bumped up a grade even though she's not exactly what you'd call...studious.

"She's gifted," Mama says proudly to the counselor. I cough.

My parents don't want me going to high school right away, even though I'm old enough and my grades qualify me.

"No," Tata says firmly. "She stay wit sistr. Dey go togeder."

"She's gifted—my dupe, my behind," I mumble under my breath so no one hears.

The only gifted one in this family is me. I'll show them who's gifted!

I don't want to be a black sheep in the family. Just because I'm different from three of them. It makes me wonder if I'm adopted. *What if my real father is not my Tata? And my mother is not my Mama? At least, being different would make sense.*

Ari might be gifted in shaking her ass and dressing like a mini fashionista. Always wearing heavy makeup. Like she doesn't think she's pretty enough. Like she doesn't see herself with the same eyes I see her. She's got the attitude, the cool factor, the ability to charm adults and classmates alike. She might be the life of a party. She might be the looks of the family...but I'm the books.

And while looks get judged by their cover, books—real books—are meant to be opened, read, and remembered.

So, I let her sparkle on the outside.

I'll win on the inside.

So now, I'm signed up to attend Kilmer Elementary—with Arijana. Great.

Just what every awkward immigrant nerd dreams of: being glued to their hot, loud, glittery sister who walks like she's on a runway and talks like she invented English.

While I'm over here looking like I just crawled out of a library fire, she's got her hair perfectly straightened with, like, one hundred butterfly clips.

I'm still figuring out what deodorant is. She struts through the hallway like she owns the place. I trip over air. And don't even get me started on lunch. She somehow always has snacks people want to trade for. I've got soggy bread in a reused butter container.

But here's the secret I'll never tell her: Sometimes I wish I was more like her. That we were the same. That we could be...besties. Like matching outfits, secret handshake, talk-about-everything kind of besties.

But instead, I'm just her slightly weird, slightly jealous sidekick with a backpack twice my size and a journal full of invisible thoughts.

Yup. Kilmer Elementary, here I come. With sparkles...and crumbs of resentment.

49

Aldi Alone

Chicago, United States of America – September 1998

A few days later, we move out of Mama's aunt's place with all the grace and glamour of war refugees on laundry day—backpacks, plastic bags, and donated blankets in tow. Basically, the same as before, only colder and with cockroaches who now speak English.

Welcome to our new life: government cheese, thrift store coats, and middle school in a language that tastes like dry crackers in my mouth.

We find an old couch on the street—dirty, ripped, shaped like it's been through a lot. We throw a red blanket over it and pretend it's new. Mama rescues a baby-blue rug from a Chicago alley (classy) and scrubs it like it personally offended her. Boom. Instant living room.

Tata lands a construction job with a Bosnian guy who probably ran from the same war. After his first paycheck, he takes us to McDonald's. A cultural milestone. I'd only seen it on TV—where it looks fun and magical. In real life, it smells like fries and existential dread.

"Please...fries, Coca-Cola, and sandwich," I mumble, sounding like a confused robot. Then I turn to Mama and whisper, "Kako se kaže piletina?" I want chicken—only chicken—because who the hell knows what's inside a hamburger here? Pork? Squirrel? Ground-up freedom?

A man behind us leans forward and asks in Bosnian, "Trebate li pomoć?"

Yes, but are you gonna poison me? He's Serb. I can tell by his accent, the way he says ćevapi like a villain. My stomach twists into origami. *Is this a trap? Is Ronald McDonald part of a conspiracy?*

Mama gives me that look, half warning, half surrender that says, *we're starving, just take the food, child.*

The guy smiles and tells the cashier, "Chicken sandwich. No pork." Then turns back assuring us that everything will be fine, "Biće dobro. Sve će biti u redu." I nod. I don't believe him. But I want to. Also...fries.

That same day, we go to Kmart. A big event. We need everything—underwear, shampoo, the will to live. Cousin Husein, MVP of our survival arc, buys us winter coats. Arijana and I pick matching reversible jackets—black on one side, silver on the other. Shiny. Dramatic. Recession-chic.

Once, in Vranduk, a relative from Germany sent us a pink-and-silver dress with matching shorts. I wore it like it was Gucci. Special occasions only: birthdays, ceasefires, Tuesdays without bombings.

Back at Kmart, Arijana disappears into the toy aisle. She's twelve. Playing with dolls like she's five. Because the war stole everything—bikes, Barbies, basic childhood.I made books out of newspaper. She played "Next Idol." I played "School." We were weird. And war-aged.

A month later, we move again. One building over. It smells like wet onions, cigarette ghosts, and mild depression. The floors creak like they've seen some shit. The radiator hisses at us like a racist cat. But hey—it's bigger. So...progress?

Then it hits, culture shock. Like being slapped in the face by America wearing a Spice Girls shirt. I cry every night under our donated blankets, grieving for a home that no longer exists.

Everything's too loud. Too bright. Too...much.

We go to Aldi, the grocery store, like we've won a game show.

Tata says, "This is heaven."

"This is survival," I respond

He's still sick. PTSD. Unspoken trauma. He watches us like we might escape. No sleepovers. No phone calls. No fun. Just school, home, repeat.

I cling to my dictionary like it's my best friend. Better than ESL—English as a Second Language—class. Golden Girls and telenovelas become my English tutors. Suzanne, Martin, The Jeffersons—all my late-night professors of American sarcasm and shade.

Still...no friends. Just subtitles. Homework. Daydreams about vanishing.

Eventually, the tears dry up. But something worse takes their place. That quiet voice. That whisper. *What if you didn't exist? What if it all just stopped?*

I get tired of feeling like I take up space I don't deserve. Of pretending I belong when everything around me keeps reminding me I don't.

This is supposed to be the dream. America, land of freedom. So why does it feel like just another war—only with better marketing?

Ari's lucky. She's got Balkan kids in her class. A Bosnian squad.

Me? I'm Kevin McCallister, minus the mansion, language skills, and cheeky one-liners. I'm alone in Rogers Park, praying someone leaves me behind on purpose.

Phone calls to Bosnia cost too much, so I write letters I never send. I journal in the notebook Cousin Husein gave me. The same day he bought us those jackets. Black and silver. Two sides. Like me. A girl split in half—Bosnia and America. Past and future.

In this new world, I learn something else: Being Black, gay, or different is hard. But there's power in it.

I watch Black kids walk like they own the world.Gay kids wear eyeliner and confidence. I don't know what it's like to be them. But I know what it's like to be stared at like a mistake.

So, I write poems. In Bosnian. About ghosts, and hunger, and survival. About trying to sew myself back together with words. Trying to quiet that sad, loud, invisible thing inside me.

I eat when I'm not hungry. Clothes don't fit. I'm soft now. Round. The second chin says hi. At first, food was comfort. Then it became shame. I feel disgusted. Like my body betrayed me. Like this life did too.

Sometimes, I wish I could go back to Bosnia.Even during the war. Because at least there, I knew who I was. Here, I'm just lost in translation.

School sucks. Girls are mean. Whispers follow me like shadows. So, I shrink. Keep quiet. Even when I know the answer, I keep my hand down. Better invisible than laughed at.

Mr. Leon, my tiny Chinese ESL teacher, tries to call my name, "Aldij-jah-nah? Aldi-hanah? Peh-lee-one-of...?" The class erupts in laughter. "Witch! Witch!" someone hisses. I want the fire drill to become a real fire. Only two kids talk to me, a boy and a girl from Albania. But our friendship is like a bad translation. I want to tell them everything—about Bosnia, the camps, the barbed wire. But my throat is locked. Like my heart forgot the code.

My parents say, "Amerikanci su ludi. Samo ludi idu kod psihologa. Mi smo preživjeli gore." Americans are crazy. Only crazy people go to psychologists. We survived up there. Cool. Good talk. So, I keep it all inside.

Anxiety.

Panic.

Flashbacks.

Shame.

Silence.

At night, I whisper to the ceiling, *Please, just let me get sick. Let it end naturally. Quietly. Let me disappear without causing trouble.*

But here's something else I never say out loud:Sometimes, when no one's home, I sneak into the bathroom and put on Ari's shiny lipstick.

Then I grab one of Mama's scarves and wrap it around my head like I'm in a music video instead of Rogers Park.

I strike a pose in the mirror—shoulders back, chin up—pretending I'm someone who isn't afraid. Someone who belongs. Someone who gets invited to school dances. Someone who flirts without blushing. Someone who matters.

And sometimes…I put on Ari's miniskirts and high heels too. Walk around the apartment like I'm headed to a party I wasn't invited to. Sometimes I even talk to the mirror in fake English, like I'm a girl from TV. Then I take it all off before anyone comes home. Because even good Bosnian girls have secrets. And this is another one of mine.

50

Good Girls, Big Secrets

Chicago, United States of America – October 1998.

Our first apartment was basically a roach convention. I swear those roaches held meetings in our kitchen.

One night, the power goes out while I'm reaching into the closet. In the dark, I step on something small and cold—a mouse. I kill it. Instantly. My heart pounds. I want to cut off my own foot. I feel like a murderer. I've never liked mice. I've always been scared of them, but this is different. I start to cry.

Tata walks in, calm as always. He helps me bury it outside. I don't know what else to do, so I recite Al-Fatiha, the prayer Nana taught me, hoping it will ease the weight in my chest.

Our second apartment on Wallen Street burns down—not our unit exactly, but the whole building catches fire one chaotic night. The smell of smoke is so thick it clings to my hair and clothes for days. Fire trucks race down the street like we're in a bad action movie, lights flashing so hard I think I've gone blind. A news reporter even interviews me about being a "brave Bosnian refugee," which is hilarious because all I want to do is vanish before I cough up a lung. The feeling is the same as war.

But worst of all is the bullying and physical assault. It's Halloween season. We've been in Chicago for about a month. Our English is minimal.

A group of big girls blocks our way home. They look like they own the street—loud, laughing, dragging their feet like they're bored and hunting for trouble. The leader is huge—easily over 300 pounds—with arms like tree trunks and the hungry eyes of a wolf. Her fake gold hoops swing like warning signs as she marches toward Ari and I.

"Where you think you goin', white girl?" she snarls, her eyes locked on Arijana's school project.

My heart drops to my toes. Her words come fast, too fast, in a thick accent I still can't decipher. It sounds like English, but not from ESL class. This is street English—rough, sharp, impossible to translate in my head.

I want to disappear. Just evaporate, like the ghosts of war. Instead, I stand frozen, backpack digging into my shoulders, cold air stinging my cheeks.

She comes closer and shoves me. For no reason. Just to show power. "What. You gonna cry, little refugee?"

That word—refugee—hits harder than her hand. She says it like it's dirty. Like I'm dirty. And maybe I am. We don't have a real home—just constant moving and secondhand everything.

"Shut up," I mumble in the most American voice I can manage, but even I hear the accent sticking out.

Then comes the slap. Fast. Hot. Pain cracks across my cheek like lightning. My vision blurs. My mouth tastes like metal. I think, *This isn't happening. Not here. Not again. I must be the main character in some Hollywood movie.*

"Give me that! Give it, white girl!" the biggest one yells.

We freeze and keep walking. "You didn't hear me, dumbass? Don't speak English? Who do you think you are?" she sneers.

I don't understand most of what she says. It's some strange dialect of English I'll never learn. I think, *Great, now I have to learn another language.*

She starts cussing us out. Her words grow more violent. I try to end it all in my head. Stars blur my vision. Then someone shouts: "Hey, you girls, that's enough! Come here!"

A short woman in a bright orange raincoat and hat appears. Even though she's smaller than them, the girls scatter in seconds. The woman hugs me and asks, "Are you okay, sweetheart? Let's call the police."

I shake my head. I'm scared. I don't know enough English to explain. "I'm OK," I say. It's strange being hugged by a stranger. In Bosnia, people don't do that unless they're family.

She tries to ask more questions, but eventually lets us go. Ari and I run the rest of the way home, crying. Once we calm down, we decide not to tell anyone. We don't know how to defend ourselves, and we're scared of what might happen. Mama agrees it's best to stay quiet. After that, she starts walking us to and from school.

I get my second kiss. This time a real one. With tongue. Wet and confusing. Like in telenovelas, just without the glamour.

Only Arijana and a few close friends know. And they better not say anything, because if someone finds out—I'm dead. Not "grounded" dead—dead-dead. Buried-under-someone's-basement-like-that-serial-killer-Gacy dead.

It happens behind the building, next to a rusty dumpster that smells like rotten cabbage and diapers. Not exactly a romantic backdrop. No roses.

No music. Just spray-painted trash with "F*** the system" and a trail of ants dragging a squashed ketchup packet.

And he's not even Bosnian. A short, dark-skinned Mexican kid who gels his hair into a helmet and always hums mariachi songs under his breath.

He's been watching me since we moved in. Not in a creepy way—more shy and respectful. He always smiles. One time he gives me gum and says, "You got pretty eyes, preciosa."

"Just one kiss," he whispers like the trash might hear us.

I glance around, heart in my throat. "If my dad finds out, he'll bury me in the laundry room."

But I let him kiss me. Once. Just once. Awkward. Wet. Quick. A little gross. A little exciting. A little... something I don't have a name for. Then I run home.

Arijana finds out because, of course, she always does. She has that annoying little-sister radar that works better than the FBI.

She doesn't say anything at first. But now she uses it as leverage.

"Maybe I'll tell Tata," she smirks when she wants the last piece of pie.

"Go ahead," I shoot back. "He'll hit you first for talking to boys on the playground."

She squints at me. "Try me."

But she knows I won't. Doesn't even need to bet. We both live under the same fear—the look on Tata's face when he gets angry. The sound of the belt coming off. The silence that follows the yelling.

One time, she went to her Nigerian friend's house after school and didn't tell anyone. When she came back a few hours later, Mama was already crying, and Tata was holding the phone, ready to call the police. He thought she'd been kidnapped or killed.

When she walked in, all innocent, they both lost it.

"Where were you?!" Mama screamed, tears streaming down her face.

"You think we escaped one war just to lose you here?!" Tata roared, pulling off his belt.

The sound of leather on skin—crack, smack, crack—echoed down the hallway.

I hid in the closet. Covered my ears. I wanted to run out and stop him, but I couldn't move. I couldn't breathe. Because if I said anything—I'd be next.

That's how it works in our house. Silence is safety. Secrets are survival. And kisses? Kisses are dangerous.

51

The Kids Are "Fine"

Chicago – Fall 1999

Once again, we move. Third apartment in a year. By now, moving felt like a weird family hobby nobody signed up for—like we were collecting addresses instead of stamps.

Our next apartment was in a "nicer" neighborhood between "Little India" and "Little Pakistan." The streets buzzed with Bollywood music, smells of spices that made my nose twitch, and shop windows glittering like movie sets.

Our new place was clean and had two bedrooms. The catch? Parking was a nightmare.

Later, Tata got his own beating—because apparently, just existing in the neighborhood was an offense.

He'd gone to ask around for a parking spot and walked past a garage full of shady guys. One of them, a tattooed man with a knife that glinted like a Halloween prop, started chasing him.

Tata, who's not exactly Olympic material, ran like his life depended on it—which it did.

Just when Tata thought he was safe, the guy caught him and punched him square in the ribs.

"Are you okay?" Mama asked when Tata limped home, clutching his side like he'd been in a wrestling match with a bear.

"Fine," Tata grunted, trying to sound tough but wincing every time he breathed.

I looked at the growing bruise on his ribs and said, "That's gonna leave a mark."

"Like a tattoo," Tata joked, trying to lighten the mood.

But it wasn't a joke. That punch was the final straw.

"We're moving again," Tata announced like it was a sentence to death.

I groaned. "Third time's the charm?"

Mama rolled her eyes. "More like the third time's the headache."

Mama's been taking care of Bosnian kids at our new place. Often, Ari and I help too. This new apartment on Oakley Street close to Devon is huge.

Our new apartment has two bedrooms, a living room, dining room, bathroom, and lots of windows. It's on the third floor, though. Our neighbors are Bosnians and Herzegovinians. It makes it easier to communicate. The owner is also Bosnian. They seem nice. Their kids are similar ages like me and Arijana.

Each month, we send money to Bosnia—to Nana Điha, Majka Zulka, and Dido Hašim.

Sometimes, I hear Mama and Tata argue about it. I don't understand. Father's tone of voice and his body language change each time they bring up Mama's side of the family. It's like there are secrets and drama. Arijana and I don't get involved. We just close our door and play loud music.

Tata finds cleaning jobs for us. Mama, Arijana, and I deep clean filthy, roachy, stinky apartments. Mama's in charge and she divides the jobs. We use our bare hands. Gloves are a luxury.

"Why waste money that we can send to Bosna," Mama says.

"She's probably right," Ari and I both conclude.

"At least we're here. Each cleaning. A step closer to the American dream."

The chemicals make me puke. After each cleaning gig, I cough for days. I sneeze, my eyes are pink and itchy, and I can't breathe. I want to ask Tata to buy us masks and gloves, but I don't want to be a spoiled brat.

You need to be grateful, that's what they would say. So, I scrub and rub like my life depends on it. Sometimes, I make myself bleed. Bruises bloom across my arms and shins like purple flowers. It's almost like I never left Bosnia—I still feel like someone is chasing me, watching me like an eagle, forcing me to run for my life.

Even though cleaning makes me physically sick, it helps me forget. The chemicals burn my throat, my eyes turn red, and I sneeze so hard my ribs hurt. But it quiets the noise in my head. Keeps my thoughts locked in on one task. Sometimes, it's even calming—the rhythm of wiping, scrubbing, rinsing. Like I can wash away the past if I just scrub hard enough.

We get paid in cash. Mama takes it without saying much, folds the bills, and slips them into her pocket. At home, she hands it to Tata, who locks it in a small black safety box hidden deep in their closet, screwed to the wall behind old winter coats. They don't trust banks. Every dollar we earn gets buried in that box like treasure.

Ari and I never see a single penny. No allowance, no wallet money. Our reward is a trip to Burger King or a "shopping spree" at a used clothing store that makes my skin itch just from walking in. On rare days—if Mama and Tata are in a good mood—they take us to Payless and let us choose a pair of sneakers or summer sandals. Brand new, still in the box. That's the jackpot.

"It's not fair that we don't get any of the cash the three of us make," Ari whispers to me at night.

"I know," I whisper back. But neither of us dares say it out loud to them.

Mama and Tata stop going to evening ESL classes at Interfaith Immigration Agency.

"Who has time to learn English when we need to support our family—both here and in Bosna," they say, almost in unison.

By now, my English is excellent. And because I'm the oldest, every piece of mail, every document, every phone call or appointment falls on me. Doctor's visits, school forms, bank papers—even job applications for them. It's all me. And sometimes, I wish I had never learned English at all. That way, maybe I wouldn't be so responsible for everyone else's life.

When I translate, I'm extra careful. Word for word. No room for mistakes. One wrong word, one misunderstood sentence, and they'll think I'm hiding something or twisting the truth.

Mama's been getting sicker. Her body's tired. She takes everything the doctors give her—pills, injections, sedatives. It's test after test. Blood draws, CAT scans, MRIs. A million-dollar workup, and still no answers. But she looks fine and she laughs whenever she's around other people. She only complains to us as if somehow it's our job to fix her. It makes me mad. Like, she's one way with everyone else, and another way with those of us at home. I can't even tell her about my pains. It's like she's the only one hurting.

I hate translating questions about her sex life. I want to disappear every time they ask. "How often do you and your husband...?" the doctor begins, and my stomach clenches. But I have no choice. I have to be the adult. I have to carry it.

Both Mama and Tata go to group therapy for Bosnian adults to talk about war trauma. Not because they want to, but because this helps us get all the government benefits. I wish we did too. I wish someone would ask how we're doing—us kids. But they don't.

"The kids are fine. They don't need therapy," they say. "They're strong. They survived. They're too young. They'll forget."

Ari looks like she's forgetting. I can't. I don't. I won't. I fear I never will.

One night, I ask Ari, "why don't they see that we need to talk about our feelings?"

She just nods, turns up the radio, and dances like she can twirl her pain away. Her feet slap the floor. The music drowns the silence.

But I lie awake at night with the questions. *What are they afraid of? Can't they see that there's something wrong with us?*

Are they scared that if we speak, it will all unravel? That we'll say something too real, something they can't handle?

Are they afraid we'll admit how broken we are?

Was it the war that did this to me—that left me depressed, anxious, hypersensitive, and aggressive—always comparing, always feeling behind? Or was I born this way? Is it in our blood, passed down like dark hair or bad teeth?

Sometimes I think, *maybe it's not the war. Maybe it's in our genes. Maybe it's generational.*

But then I stop myself. I can't blame Mama and Tata. Not them. They did what they could. What they had to. What they were taught.

So I blame everything else. The war. The world. The way we came here, broken but expected to behave.

Because if I admit it's them, then it means none of us ever stood a chance.

52

The Good Girl and the Bad One

Chicago, United States of America – Fall 1999-2002

Ari keeps getting away with things. She's mastered the art of saying, "Allahami, nisam ja"—swearing to God it wasn't her, even when she's lying through her teeth. My parents are so lost in their own heads, they often have no clue what's happening around them.

Because I'm older—and because at school I only talk to kids who follow every rule, obsess over homework like it's a survival skill, and try to make their parents proud, my parents think I'm a good girl. But they don't know those same kids are full of anxiety. They hide behind their straight A's, just like I do. We perform excellence while quietly falling apart.

They don't know that even good girls have secrets. That even good Bosnian girls have secrets—like me.

Because Mama and Tata argue about money, bills, family, and all the other grown-up stuff they don't know how to solve, Ari and I end up arguing too. A lot. They always compare us.

"Why can't you be more responsible like Aldijana?

"Why do you lie?"

"Why can't you get straight A's?

"Get a job."

"Stop asking for money," they tell sis.

"Why can't you ever be chill like Ari?"

"Why do you take everything personal?"

"Why do you read between the lines and over-analyze," they'll ask me—deleting everything nice they ever said to me before. The list never ends.

I bet Ari feels like crap when they make me sound perfect. But I'd be lying if I said I didn't like it. I live for that praise. I chase it like it's the last slice of peace I can earn.

So, I push myself to be the golden child. I don't ask to hang out with friends. I don't ask to go to Homecoming or buy a new shirt with my own money. I just do what they want. What they expect. I'm on a mission to keep them happy, to keep the peace—even if it means keeping myself on mute.

Ari? She doesn't give a shit. She does what she wants. Says what she thinks. I envy that kind of freedom. That bravery. How she can be so confident—so bold—so unapologetically herself. How she can put her needs first, when I barely know what mine even are.

Because our parents always pit us against each other, they come to me when they're upset with her.

"Talk to your sister.""Why is she acting like this?""Do something."

So, I try. I really do. I hate seeing Mama cry—especially now that she's sick. When she's sad, the whole house feels heavy, like we're all drowning and no one knows how to swim. So, I try to keep the peace. Be the bridge. The fixer. The one who absorbs the tension and smooths things over.

But Ari and I still end up fighting.

I'm stuck in the middle—again. The go-between. The peacemaker.

And when I can't take it anymore—when she rolls her eyes one too many times or calls me their little puppet—I snap.

I push her. She pushes back. One of us always ends up with bruises. Both of us end up gutted.

And when Mama and Tata find out? It doesn't matter who started it. We're both punished. Grounded. Yelled at. Hit with a belt, a hand, a wooden stick—a motka—like we're still little kids, not teenagers with real bruises on our bodies and hearts.

Last time Ari and I got physical, Mama ended up in the ER. She fainted.

We rushed her there in a panic.

"What if she's faking it," we read each other's mind. That was Mama's thing. When she couldn't control the situation, she played the victim. That was her secret.

Well—it wasn't a secret to us.

But when she did faint for real—when her lips went pale and her body went limp—we felt like monsters. Like her illness was our fault. Like we had somehow broken her.

So now, Ari and I try harder to keep our fights a secret.

Just another secret a "good girl" like me has to carry. And another bruise a "bad girl" like Ari has to hide. Even though, to me, she's not bad at all. She's just trying to survive—like I am. Only louder.

53

Forbidden Fruit, Hidden Wounds

Chicago, United States of America – Fall 1999-2002

I graduate from Kilmer Elementary School in a green cap and gown, clutching my little certificate like it's a medal. I wear a long purple dress with a giant bow—I feel like I'm in a Bollywood movie. It's a small victory, but a victory all the same.

Next is Sullivan High. Freshman year is rough but exciting. After months of awkward ESL conversations and the endless homework I assign myself, I finally exit the program. I still remember the day Mr. Leon tells me, "Aldijana, your English is almost perfect now."

I smile like I just won the lottery.

I start taking honors classes and push myself to keep straight A's. It's not easy, but it proves I belong. That summer, I land my first job as a teacher's assistant for a first-grade class. Tiny hands, nonstop questions, chaos everywhere. I love it. The kids remind me of me—curious, confused, trying to figure out the world.

I dream of becoming a teacher one day. Helping kids find their voices like I'm starting to find mine. I also dream of being a famous author. A therapist to fix myself and everyone around me. To fix this broken world I live in.

I'm a top student. A teacher's pet. A people-pleaser. I have only a few friends, and I never see them outside of school. My parents don't let me. No mall trips. No birthday parties. No life beyond books, chores, and expectations.

I translate bills. I handle insurance forms. I make doctor's appointments. I fill out job applications and read medication labels. Tata and Mama work. Ari cooks. I clean. I study. I keep the peace.

I'm the bridge between two worlds—one that raised me in war, and one that never quite feels like home.

Then Tata says, "We're moving."

"No more hauling groceries to the third floor," he grins. "It's a garden apartment. In a Croatian guy's building. Fully remodeled. Cheaper. And best of all, you'll go to Taft High. A better school."

He makes it sound like a gift. But that night, I overhear the truth.

"Why couldn't you swallow your pride?" Mama whispers. "We had to move before. Wallen Avenue. The Bosnian landlord. Now this. Again."

"Stop blaming me," Tata snaps. "You don't know what I saw in the concentration camp. What they did to me. Don't judge. They both wanted to rip me off."

Silence. I conclude that all the fighting and wars in this world are because of money.

We're not just moving because of rent. We're moving because something broke. Again.

The new place smells clean. Doesn't make me sneeze or itch. The Croatian landlord is kind. Pays Tata well. Lets us pick vegetables from his garden. Even gives us treats. He and his Polish wife become our new family.

And I learn something shocking: not all Croats are monsters. War made monsters. Not bloodlines.

Later, I take a job at another grocery store. Then another. That's where I meet him—deep brown skin, sharp eyes, perfect cheekbones. Black and Asian. He works in the freezer section. I run the register.

We like each other. He makes me laugh. Makes me feel weightless. Like maybe I deserve this—this moment of joy.

But he's the forbidden fruit. What would our people say? "She's a slut." "She's dating an Afro-Asian." "Sramota," what a shame, they'd say.

If the word got out, I swear—I don't know what I'd do. Some days I think I'd rather die than be shamed. Rather disappear than be seen as the bad Bosnian girl who dared to want something of her own.

Then one day, I slice my finger open cutting deli meat at work. Blood spills everywhere—floor, apron, arms. Someone calls 911. I get taken away in an ambulance like I've survived a warzone.

At the hospital, they stitch me up. Mama, Tata and Arijana wait. They sit with my manager just to make sure I'm okay.

And the truth is, I don't know if it was really an accident. I don't know if my hand slipped or if some hidden part of me wanted to hurt myself. Punish myself. Escape the fear of being found out.

His skin is only a little darker than Mama's. But different enough to ruin me in our community. A few weeks before the accident, during a slow shift, he kissed me in the back room. Just once. Soft. Gentle. Forbidden.

I don't tell anyone. Not even Ari. Good Bosnian girls don't kiss boys at work. Especially not boys their parents would never approve of. So, I bury it. Lock it up. Another secret layered under the others. Something no one can ever know.

Most nights, I fall asleep clutching one of my pink teddy bears that I now have a collection of.

I don't make myself bleed or give myself bruises much anymore. Only sometimes. When things get really bad. Mostly, I nap. When I nap, I don't snap.

I play soccer. I take AP classes. I never give out my phone number. Never stay late. Never go to school dances.

"Why can't I go?" I ask.

"To protect you," Tata says.

"We survived too much," Mama adds. "We don't want to lose you."

Protected. Or imprisoned?

They work. Tata drinks to be relax. Mama smokes. I stay quiet. They try. I see that. And I try too. Try to be good. Try to belong. Try to grow up in a world that never stops shifting beneath my feet.

54

Almost 18, Still Can't Breathe

Chicago, United States of America – Fall 1999–Spring 2002

I'm a senior in high school, taking all AP classes. I'm about to graduate half a semester early. I've completed every requirement, even earned some college credits. I'm on track, organized, polished—the model immigrant daughter.

Since I don't really know what a psychology or writing degree involves (and I'm pretty sure those won't pay rent), I pick teaching. Teaching feels safe. Familiar. I want to work with kids. But American elementary school is foreign to me. Middle school, especially eighth grade, still haunts me—all that puberty-fueled chaos and cafeteria trauma. No, thank you. And I hate math. So, I pick high school English. Literature. Reading. Writing. Helping kids who are learning English, like I once was.

But even with all my top grades, I only apply to one university: UIC. The one that's in our budget. I don't bother with the Ivy Leagues. Not because I couldn't get in—but because I already know I won't be allowed to go away. I've heard too many of Mama and Tata's late-night fights about money—about how much to send back home, about how Majka Zulka has two sons to help, but Nana only has Tata. I know what it costs to live in this country and still try to help everyone else survive in another. I don't want to be another burden.

I never even ask about applying anywhere else. I already know the answer. A good Bosnian girl doesn't go away for college. Why would she, unless she wants to sleep around like these lost American girls? That would be the answer, unspoken but sharp as glass. So, I keep quiet. I clip my own wings before anyone else can. But even model daughters get told to disappear.

When 9/11 happened, I was a junior at Taft. I stayed home that day with cramps, curled up under my Disney blanket. I didn't even hear about the towers until hours later. By the time I returned to school, everything had changed.

The air felt heavier. Colder. People looked at me like I was dangerous. Like I'd personally hijacked the planes. A few students asked me where I was really from. One girl whispered, "Isn't she Muslim?" like it was something that was contagious. Something she could catch off a doorknob.

Some kids even say things like Serbs and Croats should have killed all Muslims—left not a single one alive—because Bosnians were Muslim, just like Bin Laden. That whoever shares the same religion as him should be erased from the earth. The words hang in the air like poison, and suddenly, I'm not just "different," I'm a target.

My name doesn't give me away—Aldijana is ambiguous enough. But my nationality does. Everyone knows I'm Bosnian. Everyone knows I'm a refugee. That makes me other enough. And then I open my mouth and give them more reason.

They laugh every time I say a word with "th" sound. That tiny sound "th" was enough to turn into a punchline. They tease me when I read aloud in class. My tongue betrays me, words sound like they still belonged to another country. "What did she say?" "Say that again, Bosnia!" "Do you mean Thursday or Turz-day?"

Once, a boy in U.S. History coughs the word terrorist under his breath when I mispronounce Washington. No one corrects him. Not even the teacher.

At home, my parents panick. "Don't tell anyone you're Muslim," Tata said.

"Just say we're Bosnian," Mama added. "They don't have to know everything."

But I don't listen. I say it anyway. In class. In the cafeteria. In defiance. "I'm Muslim."

I don't wear a hijab. I don't pray five times a day. I don't even know all the tenets of the faith. But I am Muslim in my bones, in the way I pronounced my a's and hold grief in my jaw. And if people are going to hate me, I want it to be for the truth—not the silence my parents think will keep me safe.

Of course, there are consequences. Slurs. Locker notes. Mockery.So meone scrawls, *Go back to Bin Laden* on the bathroom stall above my backpack.

But I never take it back. I carry it all. The accent. The shame. The stubbornness. The weight of a name that never sounds quite right in anyone else's mouth.

Sometimes, I have nightmares. Of being shoved in front of the class, forced to speak while everyone laughed at how the words limped out of me. Other nights, I dream I was back behind barbed wire in Bosnia, nameless and voiceless. Some nights I dream of being dead. And as strange as it sounds, those dreams felt easier. Safer. Quieter.

Because at least the dead don't have an accent. At least the dead don't get mocked in the lunchroom, or pulled aside in airports, or watched like a threat in math class. Being dead is easier than being a child in Bosnia, behind barbed wire. But being behind barbed wire is still easier than being a lonely teenage immigrant in America, constantly mouthing the wrong words, in the wrong voice, in the wrong body.

I've only kissed a few boys—barely—but I've never had a boyfriend. That's not allowed. Tata always says, "Aldi, Ari, nema momaka dok ne napunite osamnaest!" No boyfriends until you're eighteen. Period. And I take it literally. I don't ask. I don't test it. Meanwhile, every one of my friends has a boyfriend. Some have had three. And yes, plenty of guys like me—even a few cute ones—but I'd never dare write my number on a Post-it and give it to anyone except a girl classmate. I'm almost 18, but still trapped in a glass box labeled *Good Girl*.

One day, our Bosnian Serb friends invite us to a birthday party. I want to go. Desperately. But I'm too chicken to ask. So, I bribe Ari with a $20 bill to do the dirty work.

"Please, can we go?" she begs them. "Everyone's going. They're our people—from back home! They speak our language."

Mama and Tata exchange one of their silent married-people stares. "Fine," Tata says, waving his hand like a traffic cop. "But home by ten. No drinking. No smoking."

"I don't smoke," I say quickly, eyeing Ari, who absolutely does. But she knows better than to argue—because if she doesn't follow the rules, I'll snitch, and we'll both be shipped back to Bosnia in a crate labeled Shame.

So, they let us go. And we go.

At the party, a cute Bosnian Serb boy with brown hair and piercing blue eyes walks over to me. We talk. Laugh. It's easy. Too easy. Next thing I know, his lips are pressed against mine. Soft. Warm. Like every scene in every teenage movie I'm never allowed to watch.

Then the birthday boy storms over, grabs him by the arm, eyes blazing. "Are you out of your mind? She's Muslim!" he shouts. "Muslims killed your mama and tata, and here you are kissing the first beautiful Muslim girl you meet? You better stop. Or else."

I freeze. Every inch of my body burns. Our Mexican friend, Ari's bestie and my only real friend, grabs us. "Let's get the hell out of here," she says.

We rush out. My face is wet before we hit the sidewalk. I can't stop crying. I had no idea his parents were killed by Bosniaks. I didn't know.

She's right. I know it. And now that they know what happened, I can't even use my usual threats to keep Ari in line. They have something on me. The next day at school, Ms. Dedes pulls me aside after class. She's not just a teacher—she's someone who notices when something's wrong, beyond who's Orthodox or who isn't.

I'm her favorite student. She always has me run errands for her, leave class early, help other classmates. I think she knows I pick on her Spanish mistakes, and sometimes my Spanish is even better than hers. Maybe that's why she trusts me so much. And I trust her.

"Aldijana," she says gently, "You don't have to carry the whole war on your back. Let it go. Don't complicate things. The boy. The birthday party. Your parents would lose it. Trust me."

Her words surprise me. I thought this was just between me and the others—but she sees it too. Maybe she understands that some things are bigger than religion or politics.

She's right. I know it. Now that our friend and Ari know what happened, I can't even use my usual threats to keep Ari in line. They have something on me.

So this becomes another secret a good Bosnian girl has to bury. Along with the others. Like a time capsule of shame, buried deep in the backyard of my ribs.

55

Real Friends Don't Let Friends Do Drugs

Bosnia – June 2002

Before we go back to Bosnia, I think about everything that's happened—the war, the new life in America, the secrets we carry. The past few months feel like a whirlwind. I finish high school a semester early, taking extra AP classes, pushing myself hard. I graduate in May, just weeks before I turn eighteen.

No prom for me, not because I don't want to go, but because I feel too old and too scared to ask. So instead of prom, instead of parties, we decide to fly back to Bosnia, to the place holding all our wounds and memories.

This trip becomes our celebration plan. Our way of honoring survival. A fragile attempt at reconnecting with a past both distant and unbearably close.

Mama and Tata's war trauma worsens. They grow meaner, sicker. The quiet silences in the house feel heavier, colder. Smiles come less often. Nights bring arguments that echo in my dreams.

Chicago feels like a place I live in but not quite a home. Bosnia feels like the place my heart knows, but also a place where I don't fully belong.

I'm caught between two worlds, never Bosnian enough, never American enough. Even though we have two homes, I feel homeless.

We finally have a home. A two-bedroom condo in Chicago, in a building with an elevator and a bathroom and a half. No more fighting over who gets to use the toilet.

"No more moving," Mama and Tata say. Ari and I exchange looks.

"Let's see how long we stay here before we have to pack our bags again," we whisper.

Tata works every job he can find, his hands rough and worn. We all do, cleaning apartments in the chilly Chicago suburbs, scraping together over ten thousand dollars. Enough for four plane tickets, small gifts for family, and a month of food and travel. My ticket alone costs more than a thousand. I pay for mine with money I earned tutoring and ringing up groceries, refusing to ask for a single dime.

Now, after years in America, we are finally back in Bosnia. We always said we'd return someday. The plan was to work hard, save money, then come home and rebuild. But time in exile stretches like elastic. America pulls you close, even when you don't want it to.

June, the darkest month my body remembers. The skies hang heavy, always grey. Rain falls steady, soaking into everything: cracked streets, crumbling walls, and the people moving through it all. Each drop taps a memory I try to lock away.

We're visiting for a month. Nana Điha, Majka Zulka, and Dido Hašim cry. So do we. All my aunts are here, and all my uncles—except uncle Nurija, who died a year before we moved to Chicago from tuberculosis. He caught it in a concentration camp, weakened by malnutrition and lack of food. My cousins have grown up.

One afternoon, Ado calls me upstairs with a grin I barely recognize.

"Aldi, come up. I want to show you something," he says, eyes bright but shaky.

I follow him into the attic. Dust swirls in pale sunlight slipping through a cracked skylight. Along the windowsill, pots hold rows of green, leafy plants—earthy and wild.

"What's this? Mint? Some new kind of tea you're inventing?"

He laughs, a dry bark. "Tea? You're kidding, right?"

"I'm serious."

"It's weed."

I blink. "Wait...you grow this?"

He shrugs. "Yeah. Smoke it too. Helps quiet the noise."

"Brate moj...What happened to you? You used to sketch houses on napkins. Dream about becoming an architect."

His face hardens, eyes darkening. Then he explodes.

"What happened? What happened? My dad is gone. Buried. And you—you live in America with your perfect little life, your grades and college apps. You don't get it."

"I do," I whisper. "I carry it too. But this won't help."

He pulls out a joint, lights it. "Here. Try it. Maybe you'll understand."

I shake my head. "No. But...I had a dream before we came. Your dad came to me."

He scoffs. "You're joking."

"I'm not. He said, 'Please talk to Armin. He's still a good boy. Just lost. Help him before it's too late.'"

He stares at me, as if I'm mad. Then his hands tremble. He drops the joint on the floor. Neither of us says a word.

We cry.

No words. Just grief, heavy and shared.

Back in Chicago, I used to see signs in the school bathroom: *Real friends don't let friends do drugs.*

Never thought I'd be the one standing in a dusty attic in Žepče, trying to save someone I love with nothing but a memory and a warning. Trying to save someone who doesn't want to be saved.

56

How to Become American Without Disappearing

Chicago, United States of America – 2002

Heading back to Chicago, the plane smells like sweat and disinfectant. My stomach twists into knots, but I pretend to sleep. When we land, the air feels different—cold, sharp, honest. Chicago no longer feels like exile. Not exactly. I'm caught in between—too Bosnian for America, too American for Bosnia.

On the bus, I whisper to Ari, "I don't know where I belong." She shrugs, then leans her head on my shoulder. "Me neither." We sit in silence, the city rushing past outside. "But maybe," she says softly, "it's okay not to know yet. We'll figure it out. Together."

That's when it hits me—I've spent so long trying to become American, I forgot to ask what that even means. Not on paper. Not in ceremony. But in survival. In soul.

Then, something big happens: we become U.S. citizens. I stand in a room filled with people from all over the world—headscarves, Sunday dresses, clip-on ties, nervous smiles. We raise our right hands and pledge allegiance to a country that still feels foreign, one that doesn't quite love me back yet. But here I am, trying.

Then they call my name: "Aldijana Pehlivanović." I wince. It's time. Time to shed the name that made me the butt of every joke in middle school— *"Aladdin," "Aldi-market,"* and once, *"Witch Pehlivanović,"* because apparently my last name sounded like a potion ingredient and Aldi grocery is where the poor buy food.

When they ask if I want to legally change anything, I smile wide and say, "Yes. Drop the 'j.' Aldiana. Just Aldiana." Clean. American. Easier to pronounce. Less... witchy. Still stuck with Pehlivanović though. That one's going to haunt me until marriage or death—whichever comes first.

Honestly? Some days, I wish I were a witch. I'd cast spells on every teacher who told me to go back where I came from. Curse every student who mocked my accent. Hex every boy who asked, "So...like...do you have bombs in your backpack?" Being a witch wouldn't be so bad—if it meant having even one ounce of power in a world that keeps trying to shrink me.

The thing about my accent is it's the first thing people hear. And with it comes fear—fear that I'll never sound right, never truly belong. The dead don't have accents. They don't have to explain themselves. But I do. Every day. At school, at work, even just ordering coffee. My hands sweat so badly when I shake someone's hand that I sometimes wish I could disappear.

And then there's school. I don't get bad grades because I'm not smart—I kill myself with notes, study guides, practicing speeches over and over, just to hide the fact that I don't always understand my teachers. The fear of not keeping up, of being "less than," pushes me harder than anyone knows.

So, here's what I've learned. Not from a textbook. Not from a flag. But from living between two worlds.

How to Become American Without Disappearing:

Remember who you are. Before America. Beneath the accent. Behind the smile.

Be proud of your past—even if it's painful.

Don't lie about your heritage or religion. Even when hiding is easier.

Don't lie to yourself. You don't need to be perfect to be worthy.

Stop trying to please everyone. That includes your family, friends, and society.

Do your best, and treat others how you want to be treated.

Don't hate. Don't carry grudges. Forgive—but don't forget.

Don't try to do it all alone.

Ask for help. That's strength, not weakness.

It's okay to say no. Set boundaries. Protect your peace.

Do what you can. Let go of what you can't.

You can't fix everyone. You can only change yourself.

Don't shrink your dreams just to fit in.

Dream big—and don't let anyone stop you.

Don't settle for less than what you deserve.

You can have it all. Your brain can change. You can heal.

Be kind—but don't let people use your kindness against you.

Embrace your imperfections—your accent, your scars, your difference.

Think with your own brain. You weren't made to blend in. You were made to stand out.

Trust in something bigger than yourself. A Creator. A plan. Even when it hurts.

I will be the first to go to therapy. The first to say, "This is not okay." Because getting help isn't a sign of being crazy—it's a sign of strength.

Just because someone looks fine on the outside doesn't mean they are fine on the inside. I want to break the silence, not just survive it. I want to learn how to cry without shame. I want to feel joy without guilt.

Tata still calls himself an atheist. "God's just a fairy tale," he says, lighting a cigarette. But I've seen miracles keep us alive.

Mama never prays salah because she never learned how, but she mutters duas through tears. She still flinches when the phone rings too late or the hospital calls again. Every diagnosis cracks her a little more.

They don't speak English—not really. I fill out forms, translate letters, book appointments, argue with landlords, interpret at pharmacies. I become their voice while mine gets buried under duty.

At eighteen, I'm still treated like a child who knows nothing, but I'm also the adult expected to fix everything. I walk a tightrope between invisible and indispensable.

And yet—I keep going. I keep dreaming. Because even big girls have secrets.

My biggest secret? Sometimes, even now, I still feel jealous of the dead—because being dead feels easier than being a survivor carrying scars no one can see. Hiding behind the smile.

But I choose life. I choose to smile. That's the biggest gift I can give the world—not just surviving—but truly living.

I want to find out who I am beyond the trauma, beyond the fear, beyond Bosnia, beyond Chicago.

One day, I'll wake up without flinching at footsteps. One day, I'll speak without first translating myself. One day, I'll feel whole.

I want to grow. I want to heal. I want to live a life my younger self never dared to dream of. And this time, I believe I can.

I close my eyes and breathe in the quiet. I don't have all the answers. I don't know where the road will lead. But I know this—no matter how many doors close, new ones will open.

Seeds must fall and die before new life can grow. Some things we don't get to choose—not because we don't deserve them, but because life has a plan. Other times, we do get to choose. So, I will keep my heart open. I will leave doors open—for hope, for healing, for becoming, for myself.

Because maybe, just maybe, that is how we find who we were always meant to be.

And sometimes, when no one's looking—I wish I had the power to rise above it all. To confront the cruelty. To uncover the truth. To rewrite my story on my own terms.

And finally—to breathe.

Indeed, with hardship comes ease. —Qur'an 94:6

From the Author

Thank you for reading Jealous of the Dead.
I would highly appreciate if you write a review with your thoughts.

Please connect with me:
Instagram: aldiana_deumic
Facebook: Aldiana Deumic